Harold R Foster

Prince Valiant

COMPRISING PAGES 1005 THROUGH 1050

The Kings Of Cornwall

FANTAGRAPHICS BOOKS

ABOUT THIS EDITION:

Produced in cooperation with the Danish publisher Interpresse and several other publishers around the world, this new edition of PRINCE VALIANT is intended to be the definitive compilation of Hal Foster's masterpiece.

In addition to this volume, Fantagraphics has in stock nineteen more collections of Foster's Prince Valiant work (Vols. 5-22 and 26). The ultimate goal is to have the entirety of Hal Foster's epic, comprising 40 volumes, in print at once.

ABOUT THE PUBLISHER:

FANTAGRAPHICS BOOKS has dedicated itself to bringing readers the finest in comic book and comic strip material, both new and old. Its "classics" division includes *The Complete E.C. Segar Popeye*, the *Complete Little Nemo in Slumberland* hardcover collection, and *Pogo* and *Little Orphan Annie* reprints. Its "modern" division is responsible for such works as Yellow Kid Award-winner *Love and Rockets* by Los Bros. Hernandez, Peter Bagge's *Hate*, Daniel Clowes's *Eightball*, and American editions of work by Muñoz & Sampayo, Alberto Breccia, and F. Solano Lopez, as well as *The Complete Crumb Comics*.

PREVIOUS VOLUMES IN THIS SERIES:

PRINCE VALIANT, Volume 23
"THE KINGS OF CORNWALL"
comprising pages 1005 (May 13, 1956) through 1050 (March 24, 1957)
Published by Fantagraphics Books, 7563 Lake City Way NE, Seattle, WA 98115
Editorial Co-Ordinator: Pia Christensen
Colored by Montse Serra of Bardon Art, S.A.
Cover inked by Mårdøn Smet and colored by Montse Serra
Fantagraphics Books staff: Kim & Mark Thompson
Copyright ©1995 King Features Syndicate, Inc., Bull's, Interpresse, & Fantagraphics Books, Inc.
Printed in Denmark
ISBN 1-56097-158-4
First Printing: Winter, 1995

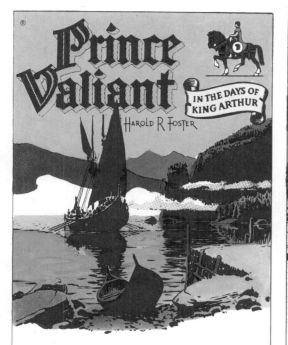

Prince Valiant
IN THE DAYS OF KING ARTHUR
HAROLD R. FOSTER

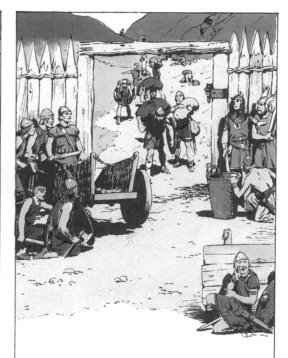

Our Story: WHEN THE MISTS OF DAWN LIFT, A SHIP DRAWS INTO THE STRONGHOLD OF GUNNAR FREYSSON, AND ARMED WARRIORS DISEMBARK.

AND PRINCE VALIANT ORDERS THAT THE WOMEN AND CHILDREN BE HERDED DOWN THE BEACH OUT OF HARM'S WAY.

THEN THEY WAIT BEHIND THE PALISADE FOR THE RETURN OF THE RAIDERS.

WEARIED BEYOND ENDURANCE BY THEIR LONG STRUGGLE ACROSS THE SNOWY MOUNTAINS, THEY SUBMIT WITH HARDLY A WOUND. ALL EXCEPT GUNNAR FREYSSON AND HIS SON, HELGI!

KNOWING THE CRUEL FATE THEIR RAID HAS EARNED THEM, THEY PREFER TO DIE FIGHTING. BOTH DRAW THEIR WEAPONS AND SPRING AT VAL!

WITH MERCIFUL SWIFTNESS VAL CUTS DOWN HIS TWO EXHAUSTED ATTACKERS. "BETTER TO BE A BUTCHER THAN WITNESS THE SLOW AND HORRIBLE DEATH THEIR DEEDS HAVE MERITED," HE MUTTERS.

BUT THE SIGHT OF BLOOD INFLAMES HIS MEN AND HE IS HARD PUT TO PREVENT THEM FROM PUTTING THE PRISONERS TO THE SWORD. "HOLD!" HE CRIES. "THESE ARE THE MEN WHO ARE TO REBUILD WHAT THEY HAVE DESTROYED!"

NEXT WEEK:- A Debt Paid.

1005 5-13-56

Prince Valiant

IN THE DAYS OF KING ARTHUR

by Harold R Foster

Our Story: EARL JON AND HIS MEN ARE BALKED IN THEIR THIRST FOR VENGEANCE. "WHAT GOOD CAN COME OF SLAYING HELPLESS PRISONERS?" ASKS PRINCE VALIANT. "THEY DID BUT FOLLOW THE COMMANDS OF A CRUEL AND RUTHLESS LEADER. THEY WILL KNOW THE KING'S JUSTICE!"

THE PRISONERS ARE SET TO WORK LOADING THE SHIP WITH THE PLUNDER THEY TOILED SO HARD TO BRING ACROSS THE MOUNTAINS.

THEN, TO THEIR SORROW, THEY ARE SENT UNDER GUARD TO RETURN THE WAY THEY CAME, TO RETRIEVE LOOT ABANDONED ALONG THE TRAIL.

GUNDAR HARL, THE CRIPPLED BUILDER OF SHIPS, AT LONG LAST RECEIVES HIS REWARD FROM VAL: "NOW THAT GUNNAR FREYSSON HAS GONE TO HIS DUBIOUS REWARD, I GIVE YOU THIS FIEF TO HOLD IN THE KING'S NAME!"

TREES ARE FELLED AND TIMBERS HEWN. EARL JON'S HALL WILL BE RESTORED ERE WINTER COMES, FOR NEVER DID MEN WORK HARDER THAN THESE PRISONERS. THE MEN THEY HAVE SO SORELY WRONGED STAND GUARD WITH BITTER EYES AND READY WEAPONS.

ALETA HAS LONG SINCE RETURNED TO VIKINGSHOLM; FOR WHAT PRETTY WOMAN WANTS TO PROLONG A VISIT WHEN ALL HER FINE DRESSES ARE BURNT TO ASHES?

1006 5-20-56

AND VAL COMES HOME TO A WORRIED WIFE. "PRINCE ARN IS WITH THE KING, PLANNING A FEAT BEYOND HIS YEARS. PLEASE RESTRAIN HIM!"

"YOUR MAJESTY, THE FERTILE VALLEYS MY SIRE DISCOVERED ARE USELESS WITHOUT A ROAD. GARM AND I WISH TO FIND A WAY FOR THAT ROAD!"

NEXT WEEK:- The Surveyors.

HAL FOSTER

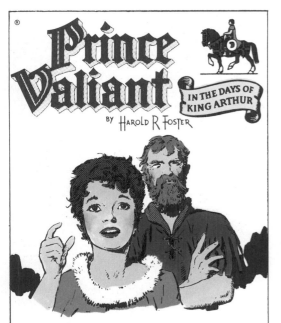

Prince Valiant

IN THE DAYS OF KING ARTHUR

BY HAROLD R FOSTER

Our Story: PRINCE ARN IS PLEADING WITH THE KING :— "A WAY MUST BE FOUND TO MAKE ACCESSIBLE THE RICH FARM LANDS MY SIRE DIS-COVERED. GARM AND I WISH TO FIND THAT WAY THROUGH THE MOUNTAINS."

"BUT, ARN, WINTER IS NIGH, ALREADY THE PEAKS ARE COVERED WITH SNOW, THERE WILL BE DANGER AND HARD-SHIP!" PROTESTS THE KING.

"IF I AM TO COMMAND MEN, THEN I MUST LEARN TO COMMAND MYSELF! HOW BETTER CAN I LEARN THAN FROM THE RESPONSIBILITY OF THIS PROJECT?"

AS VAL ADVISES HIS SON TO BE CAREFUL AND AVOID DANGER, HE REMEMBERS HIS FATHER HAD ONCE GIVEN HIM THE SELFSAME ADVICE, AND HE HAD GONE HIS OWN HEADSTRONG, INDEPENDENT WAY.

ALETA TAKES GARM'S BONY HAND AND SAYS NOT A WORD. "I KNOW, LADY QUEEN," SAYS GARM, "ARN IS CUT FROM THE SAME PATTERN AS HIS PARENTS AND CANNOT BE TURNED FROM HIS PURPOSE. I WILL GUIDE HIS STEPS. TRUST ME."

VAL AND ALETA WATCH THEM GO. THE LAKE LOOKS WILDER, THE ROCKY CLIFFS MORE THREATENING AND THE DISTANT MOUNTAINS A SILENT MENACE, NOW THAT THEIR SMALL SON IS AMONG THEM

HAL FOSTER

1007 5-27-56

ONLY ONCE DOES ARN LOOK BACK AND WAVE. THEN HE TURNS EAGER EYES AHEAD WHERE LIES THE UNKNOWN— ADVENTURE, FAILURE OR SUCCESS !

NEXT WEEK :—**Easy Going.**

Prince Valiant

IN THE DAYS OF KING ARTHUR

BY HAROLD R FOSTER

Our Story: PRINCE ARN AND GARM SET OUT TO FIND A ROUTE OVER WHICH A ROAD MIGHT BE BUILT TO REACH THE RICH FARMLANDS IN THE INTERIOR.

THEY TRAVEL BY WATER AS FAR AS THEIR LIGHT SKIFF WILL GO.

THE UPTURNED SKIFF OFFERS THE LAST SHELTER THEY ARE TO KNOW FOR MANY A LONG DAY.

GARM, THE HUNTER, IS WISE IN THE WAYS OF THE WILD, SO THEY TRAVEL LIGHT.

ON A SHEET OF PARCHMENT, RULED IN SQUARES, THEY CAREFULLY TRACE EACH DAYS PROGRESS. FOR ARN THIS IS SERIOUS BUSINESS AND A RECORD MUST BE KEPT.

ONE AFTER ANOTHER THE VALLEYS ARE EXPLORED...AND EACH ONE BEGINS SO PROMISINGLY.....

1008 6-3-56

.....BUT ENDS IN A WILD CHAOS OF CLIFFS AND TUMBLED STONE. NOT ONE LEADS TO A PASS OVER THE MOUNTAINS!

HAL FOSTER

LIKE A TRUE SON OF PRINCE VALIANT, ARN IS AT HIS BEST WHEN FACED WITH SURE DEFEAT. *"WAKE UP, GARM. I HAVE AN IDEA!"*

NEXT WEEK:—A Point of View.

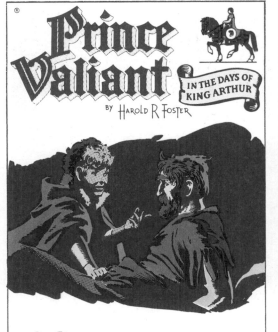

Prince Valiant
IN THE DAYS OF KING ARTHUR
BY HAROLD R. FOSTER

Our Story: IN THE DARKEST HOUR OF DEFEAT PRINCE ARN GETS AN IDEA AND SHAKES GARM AWAKE. GARM LISTENS CAREFULLY, NODS HIS HEAD, THEN GOES BACK TO SLEEP.

"FIRST WE MUST FIND A PASS OVER THE MOUNTAINS BEFORE US, SO LET US CLIMB THE MOUNTAIN BEHIND, THAT WE MAY VIEW THE WHOLE RANGE."

AS THEY CLIMB, THE COUNTRY BELOW CAN BE SEEN IN MORE AND MORE DETAIL, LIKE A HUGE MAP.

THE LAST PART OF THE CLIMB IS DANGEROUS IN THE SNOW, FOR WINTER HAS ALREADY COME TO THE MOUNTAINTOPS.

"THERE IS OUR PASS!" CRIES ARN. "SEE THAT SADDLE BETWEEN THE HIGH PEAKS? NO HIGH MOUNTAINS APPEAR BEHIND IT, SO IT MUST BE THE WAY THROUGH!"

ARN IS GLAD TO GET BACK TO CAMP AND WARM HIMSELF, FOR HE HAD BECOME CHILLED TO THE BONE ON THE MOUNTAINTOP.

GARM HAD SAVED THE HIDES OF ALL THE GAME THEY HAD EATEN. EACH EVENING HE HAD CUT AND STITCHED ON A SURPRISE FOR ARN.

AND A PLEASANT SURPRISE! AS THEY BEGIN THEIR CLIMB TO THE PASS ARN FEELS READY TO MEET THE CHILL OF HIGH PLACES.

NEXT WEEK:- The Obstacle.

HAL FOSTER

1009 6-10-56

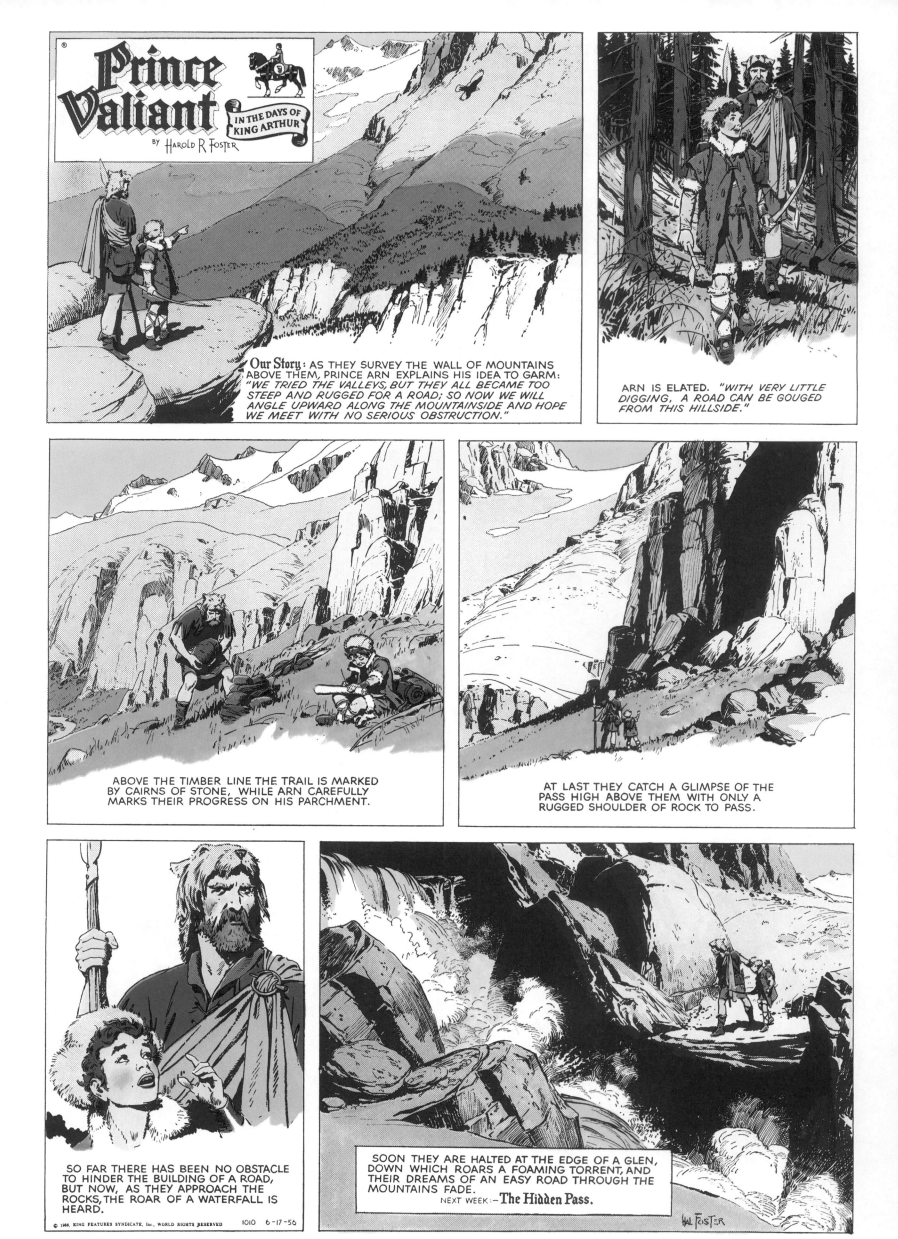

Our Story: AS THEY SURVEY THE WALL OF MOUNTAINS ABOVE THEM, PRINCE ARN EXPLAINS HIS IDEA TO GARM: "WE TRIED THE VALLEYS, BUT THEY ALL BECAME TOO STEEP AND RUGGED FOR A ROAD; SO NOW WE WILL ANGLE UPWARD ALONG THE MOUNTAINSIDE AND HOPE WE MEET WITH NO SERIOUS OBSTRUCTION."

ARN IS ELATED. "WITH VERY LITTLE DIGGING, A ROAD CAN BE GOUGED FROM THIS HILLSIDE."

ABOVE THE TIMBER LINE THE TRAIL IS MARKED BY CAIRNS OF STONE, WHILE ARN CAREFULLY MARKS THEIR PROGRESS ON HIS PARCHMENT.

AT LAST THEY CATCH A GLIMPSE OF THE PASS HIGH ABOVE THEM WITH ONLY A RUGGED SHOULDER OF ROCK TO PASS.

SO FAR THERE HAS BEEN NO OBSTACLE TO HINDER THE BUILDING OF A ROAD, BUT NOW, AS THEY APPROACH THE ROCKS, THE ROAR OF A WATERFALL IS HEARD.

SOON THEY ARE HALTED AT THE EDGE OF A GLEN, DOWN WHICH ROARS A FOAMING TORRENT, AND THEIR DREAMS OF AN EASY ROAD THROUGH THE MOUNTAINS FADE.
NEXT WEEK:—The Hidden Pass.

1010 6-17-56

Prince Valiant

IN THE DAYS OF KING ARTHUR

BY Harold R. Foster

Our Story: PRINCE ARN AND GARM STAND BESIDE A ROARING TORRENT. FOR WEEKS THEY HAVE BEEN SEARCHING FOR A ROUTE ON WHICH TO BUILD A ROAD OVER THE MOUNTAINS, AND NOW THIS CHASM BARS THEIR WAY.

THEY FOLLOW UP THE STREAM SEEKING A CROSSING AND ENTER THE CLEFT IN THE MOUNTAINS FROM WHICH THE STREAM ISSUES.

BEYOND THE CLEFT A BEAUTIFUL MEADOW AND LAKE LIE CUPPED BY TOWERING CLIFFS. *"WE WILL HAVE TO WALK AROUND THAT LAKE IF WE ARE TO REACH THE OTHER SIDE,"* SAYS GARM.

AT THE FAR END OF THE LAKE THEY FIND A CURIOUS THING. ANOTHER STREAM LEAVES THE LAKE AND IT IS FLOWING IN THE OTHER DIRECTION !

ARN IS SO EXCITED HE FAIRLY RUNS DOWN THE NEW STREAM. *"WATER RUNS DOWNHILL,"* HE CRIES. *"THIS MEADOW MUST BE THE VERY TOP OF A PASS THROUGH THE MOUNTAINS !"*

1011 6-24-56

FOR ONE DARK MOMENT IT LOOKS AS IF THEIR WAY IS BLOCKED AGAIN.

HAL FOSTER

BUT ARN, SEARCHING DESPERATELY FOR A WAY OUT OF THE PASS, MAKES A DISCOVERY !

NEXT WEEK - Success and its Price.

Prince Valiant
IN THE DAYS OF KING ARTHUR
BY Harold R. Foster

Our Story: PRINCE ARN SHOUTS, AND BY THE SOUND OF HIS VOICE GARM KNOWS SUCCESS HAS AT LAST CROWNED THEIR WEEKS OF TOIL.

BELOW THEM STRETCH MILES OF FERTILE PLAIN AWAITING THE FARMER'S PLOW.... AND THEY HAVE FOUND A FEASIBLE ROUTE ON WHICH TO REACH IT WITH A ROAD.

IT SEEMS AS THOUGH THEIR SURVEY WILL BE COMPLETE IN A FEW HOURS. AS THEY WORK THEIR WAY DOWN THE SLOPE GARM MARKS THE WAY WITH CAIRNS, WHILE ARN CAREFULLY MARKS HIS MAP.

SUDDENLY GREAT CLOUDS ROLL OVER THE HEIGHTS BEHIND THEM, BLOTTING OUT THE SUN, AND AN OMINOUS WIND MOANS AMONG THE PEAKS.

"HASTEN, YOUNG MASTER!" URGES GARM, AS THE FIRST FLAKES COME HISSING DOWN. "WE MUST REACH THE SHELTER OF THE TREES IN THE PASS. IT WOULD BE FATAL TO GET TRAPPED BY SNOW ON THIS SIDE OF THE MOUNTAINS!"

SOON THE GROUND IS WHITE WITH SNOW AND THEY WOULD CERTAINLY HAVE BECOME LOST WERE IT NOT FOR THE MARKERS.

WHILE STEPPING OVER A TINY BROOK ARN SLIPS. AT ANY OTHER TIME THIS MIGHT BE FUNNY, BUT NOW IT ONLY FILLS GARM WITH DREAD.

IT WILL TAKE MORE THAN AN HOUR TO REACH SHELTER. THE WIND IS BITTER COLD. ALREADY ARN IS SHIVERING. THE LIFE OF A FUTURE KING OF THULE IS IN GARM'S HANDS

HAL FOSTER

NEXT WEEK **Death and Life.**

1012 7-1-56

Prince Valiant

IN THE DAYS OF KING ARTHUR

BY HAROLD R FOSTER

Our Story: GARM KNEELS BESIDE THE BROOK AND HOLDS PRINCE ARN WITHIN THE FOLDS OF HIS CLOAK. ALREADY HIS YOUNG MASTER IS DANGEROUSLY CHILLED, AND THE ICY FINGERS OF FEAR CLUTCH HIS STOUT HEART.

UNLACING HIS JERKIN HE HOLDS THE BOY AGAINST HIS OWN WARM BODY AND WRINGS OUT HIS GARMENTS AS DRY AS POSSIBLE.

GARM GOES AHEAD, LEANING AGAINST THE BITING WIND AND TRAMPING A PATH THROUGH THE DEEPENING SNOW. SOON EVEN THEIR STONE MARKERS ARE BURIED.

ARN STRUGGLES BRAVELY ON. EACH TIME HE STUMBLES HE RISES MORE AND MORE SLOWLY. EVEN AT THE BRINK OF EXHAUSTION GARM DOES NOT HELP HIM, FOR WELL HE KNOWS THAT ONLY HIS DESPERATE EFFORTS ARE KEEPING HIM FROM FREEZING!

ARN IS DIMLY AWARE THAT THEY ARE NO LONGER CLIMBING. THE GROUND SEEMS LEVEL. HAVE THEY AT LEAST REACHED THE PASS? THEN, THROUGH THE SWIRLING SNOW, HE SEES GARM'S RIGHT ARM DRAW BACK. THE HEAVY SPEAR FLASHES ON ITS WAY INTO THE MURK!

HE STAGGERS FORWARD AND COMES UPON GARM DEFTLY CUTTING OPEN A DEER. HE REMOVES THE ENTRAILS....

.....AND INTO THE HOT BODY CAVITY HE PLACES ARN. THEN HE WRAPS BOTH IN HIS CLOAK AND COVERS THEM WITH SNOW TO RETAIN THE HEAT. FAINTLY, AT A DISTANCE, GARM SEES A GROVE OF TREES THAT MAY OFFER SHELTER.

NEXT WEEK:— Survival.

1013 7-8-56

HAL FOSTER

Prince Valiant

IN THE DAYS OF KING ARTHUR

BY HAROLD R. FOSTER

Our Story: WITH PRINCE ARN WRAPPED UP BESIDE THE WARM BODY OF THE SLAIN DEER, HE IS IN NO DANGER OF FREEZING, AND GARM HAS ABOUT TWO HOURS TO FIND SHELTER.

AMID THE HUGE BOULDERS OF A ROCKFALL BENEATH A CLIFF GARM FINDS A SHELTERED NOOK.

HIGH OVERHEAD THE WIND ROARS AMONG THE PEAKS, WHILE IN THE SHELTERED PASS THE SNOW LAYS AN EVER-MOUNTING BLANKET OF WHITE.

EVEN BEFORE THE ROOF IS FINISHED IT IS COVERED DEEP WITH SNOW.

NOW GARM TAKES HIS STRIKING IRON AND FLINT AND STRIKES A SPARK. SOON HE HAS NURSED A TINY FLAME INTO A CRACKLING BLAZE.

THEN HE SETS OUT TO FIND ARN. OMINOUS TRACKS IN THE SNOW SEND HIM BOUNDING FORWARD, PRAYING HE IS NOT TOO LATE.

THE SCENT OF BLOOD HAS BROUGHT THE WOLVES FROM THEIR SHELTER, AND CAUTIOUSLY THEY MOVE FORWARD TOWARD THE MOUND OF SNOW WHERE ARN AND THE DEER ARE BURIED.

NEXT WEEK:- The Long Vigil.

HAL FOSTER

1014 7-15-56

Prince Valiant

IN THE DAYS OF KING ARTHUR

BY HAROLD R. FOSTER

Our Story: GREY SHAPES LOOM OUT OF THE VEIL OF SWIRLING SNOW AND CREEP TOWARD THE MOUND OF SNOW WHERE PRINCE ARN LIES BURIED.

THEN ANOTHER SHAPE TAKES FORM, AND GARM'S HEAVY SPEAR BRINGS DOWN THE NEAREST WOLF. THE OTHERS FADE AWAY, SILENTLY, AS THEY HAD COME.

AND GARM GIVES A SIGH OF RELIEF AS HE UNCOVERS HIS YOUNG MASTER. ARN IS SLEEPING, AND HIS ROSY CHEEKS ATTEST THAT HE IS WARM. ALL EXCEPT THE TIP OF HIS NOSE.... WHICH IS FROZEN.

GARM LEADS THE WAY BACK TO THE SHELTER HE HAD BUILT, CARRYING THE DEER, WHOSE WARM BODY HAD SAVED ARN FROM FREEZING TO DEATH.

WITHIN THE SHELTER IT IS WARM AND ARN'S FROST-BITTEN NOSE THAWS. HE IS ASTONISHED THAT SUCH A SMALL THING CAN HURT SO MUCH !

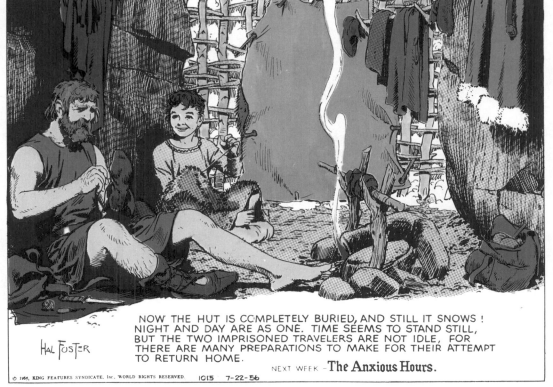

AND STILL THE BITTER STORM ROARS OVER THE MOUNTAINS, AND THE SNOW BECOMES EVER DEEPER IN THEIR SHELTERED VALLEY. THEY CUT A SUPPLY OF FUEL AGAINST THE TIME WHEN EVEN THE TREES WILL BE COVERED.

HAL FOSTER

NOW THE HUT IS COMPLETELY BURIED, AND STILL IT SNOWS ! NIGHT AND DAY ARE AS ONE. TIME SEEMS TO STAND STILL, BUT THE TWO IMPRISONED TRAVELERS ARE NOT IDLE, FOR THERE ARE MANY PREPARATIONS TO MAKE FOR THEIR ATTEMPT TO RETURN HOME.

NEXT WEEK — The Anxious Hours.

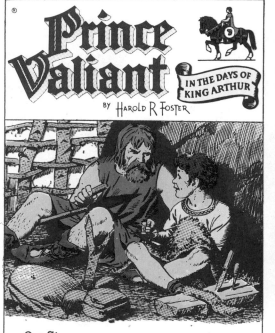

Our Story: STILL THE SNOW FALLS, AND IN THE TWILIGHT OF THEIR BURIED SHELTER GARM KEEPS PRINCE ARN EVER BUSY, THAT HE MAY NOT HAVE TIME TO THINK OF THEIR DUBIOUS FUTURE.

PRINCE ARN'S SNOWSUIT, MADE FROM THE UNTANNED WOLFSKIN, IS STIFF AND SCRATCHY, BUT IT WILL SERVE THE PURPOSE. SUDDENLY THEY LOOK UP..... A SHAFT OF SUNLIGHT POURS THROUGH THE SMOKE HOLE. THE STORM IS OVER!

DIGGING THEIR WAY OUT THEY FIND A WORLD OF BLINDING WHITE AND BITTER COLD.

BUT FOOD IS LOW AND THEY MUST BE ON THEIR DIFFICULT WAY. ARN'S FROSTBITTEN NOSE IS GREASED, HIS FACE BLACKENED, WHILE GARM FASHIONS A PAIR OF EYESHADES TO WARD AGAINST SNOW BLINDNESS.

NOW BEGINS THE GRIM STRUGGLE THAT MUST NOT CEASE UNTIL THEY REACH THE SHELTER OF THE TIMBER LINE.

WHEN THE LAKE IS REACHED GARM SIGHS WITH RELIEF. IT IS FROZEN SOLID AND THE SNOW HAS BEEN BLOWN OFF BY THE WIND; FOR ONE PRECIOUS MILE THE WAY IS EASY.

LEAVING THE PASS THEY FLOUNDER DOWN THE TREACHEROUS MOUNTAIN SIDE. THE SHORT NORTHERN DAY ENDS.

BOTH ARE EXHAUSTED WHEN AT LAST THE TIMBER IS REACHED. BUT THERE IS NO REST, FOR A SHELTER MUST BE MADE. IN THE LONG WINTER TWILIGHT ANOTHER BATTLE FOR EXISTENCE BEGINS.

NEXT WEEK:- Heartaches.

Prince Valiant

IN THE DAYS OF KING ARTHUR
BY Harold R. Foster

Our Story: IN THE FAR NORTH NIGHT IS BUT A LONG TWILIGHT, AND THE STARS, REFLECTING ON THE SNOW, GIVE GARM ENOUGH LIGHT TO FELL TWO TALL SPRUCE ACCURATELY, ONE ON TOP OF THE OTHER.

OUT OF THE TANGLED MASS OF BRANCHES GARM AND PRINCE ARN HEW A SHELTER, WEAVING THE CUT-OFF BRANCHES INTO ROOF AND WALLS. THEN THEY LIGHT A FIRE.

ARN IS RIDING HIGH ON THIS, HIS GREATEST ADVENTURE! WHAT STORIES HE'LL HAVE TO TELL HIS PARENTS!

SAFE AND WARM WITHIN THE WALLS OF VIKINGSHOLM VAL AND ALETA WATCH THE SNOW PILE HIGHER FOR FIVE LONG DAYS.

IT IS REASSURING TO SIT WITH ALETA AS SHE PRATTLES CHEERFULLY ON AND ON. SHE SEEMS NOT TO WORRY ABOUT ARN'S PERIL. CAN IT BE THAT SHE HAS NO HEART AT ALL?

WHEN SHE HAS RETIRED VAL GOES TO HIS FATHER, AND THE KING, WHO TAKES ALL THINGS QUIETLY, SAYS:— *"DON'T WORRY TOO MUCH. WE ARE A HARDY BREED AND SURVIVE MANY DANGERS, AS I KNOW ALL TOO WELL!"* THERE IS A LUMP IN VAL'S THROAT, TEARS IN HIS EYES AS HE BLURTS OUT: *"OH, FATHER, HOW OFTEN HAVE I PUT YOU THROUGH THIS TORMENT?"*

WHEN THE STORM ENDS VAL LABORS DESPERATELY, TRYING NOT TO REMEMBER ......AND AT DAYS END......

1017 8-5-56

......HE SURPRISES ALETA AT AN OPEN WINDOW. SHE IS GAZING AT THE DISTANT MOUNTAINS WHERE HER SON IS, HER WHITE FACE WET WITH TEARS.

HAL FOSTER

AND ON THOSE DISTANT MOUNTAINS A TIRED YOUNG PRINCE SLEEPS PEACE-FULLY. WITH GARM TO PROTECT HIM, AND HIS PARENTS SAFELY WITHIN CASTLE WALLS, WHAT HAS HE TO WORRY ABOUT?

NEXT WEEK:— The Ski-Maker.

Prince Valiant
IN THE DAYS OF KING ARTHUR
BY HAROLD R FOSTER

Our Story: IT IS NOT SO COLD IN THE SHELTER OF THE FOREST AS ON THE MOUNTAIN PASS, BUT THE SNOW LIES DEEP AND SOFT. GARM LEAVES PRINCE ARN TO TEND THE PRECIOUS FIRE, AND FLOUNDERS OFF THROUGH THE SNOW.

HOURS LATER HE FINDS A TREE OF THE SHAPE AND KIND HE HAS BEEN SEARCHING FOR. THEN HE CALLS ARN.

WORKING TOGETHER THEY QUICKLY HEW THE LOG FLAT.

GARM CUTS A SLOT IN THE BUTT OF THE LOG, INSERTS THE WEDGES AND CAREFULLY DRIVES THEM HOME.

BEFORE THE DAY ENDS SEVERAL PLANKS HAVE BEEN SPLIT FROM THE LOG, AND THEY HAUL THEM BACK TO THE CAMP.

BY MOONLIGHT THE SKIS ARE SHAPED AND SCRAPED. TIME IS RUNNING OUT FOR THEM...FOOD IS GETTING LOW, HUNTING IS IMPOSSIBLE.

1018   8-12-56

HAL FOSTER

THEN THEY MOVE INTO THE SHELTER WHERE GARM CEMENTS STRIPS OF DEER HIDE ON THE BOTTOM OF THE SKIS WITH MELTED SPRUCE-BALSAM WHILE ARN LACES THEM TAUT. ONLY WHEN THE WORK IS COMPLETE DO THEY TURN IN FOR THE REST OF THE NIGHT.

NEXT WEEK:- The Schuss.

Prince Valiant
IN THE DAYS OF KING ARTHUR
BY HAROLD R. FOSTER

Our Story: GARM HAS NO TIME TO INSTRUCT PRINCE ARN IN THE USE OF THEIR CRUDELY MADE SKIS, FOR NOW TIME MUST BE MEASURED BY THE AMOUNT OF FOOD AGAINST THE DISTANCE TO BE TRAVELED

NO LONGER DO THEY FLOUNDER WAIST-DEEP, BUT GLIDE EASILY ON TOP OF THE SNOW. TOO EASILY, FOR, FOLLOWING IN GARM'S SMOOTH TRACKS, ARN CATCHES UP FAR TOO OFTEN.

HE IS SHOWN HOW TO USE HIS STAFF AS A BRAKE.

NOW THEY FACE ANOTHER PROBLEM. ON THE LOWER SLOPES SUN AND WIND HAVE FORMED A HARD CRUST, AND GARM HAS DIFFICULTY BREAKING A TRAIL.

ARN MAKES A MISSTEP! UNABLE TO STOP, HE GLIDES DOWN AT A BREATH-TAKING SPEED.

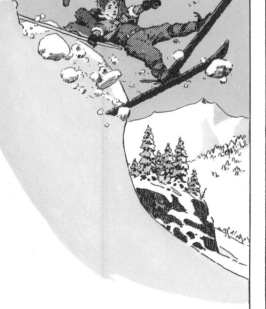

IN THOSE FAR-OFF DAYS THE SKI WAS USED ONLY AS A SNOWSHOE. MANY CENTURIES WERE TO PASS BEFORE THEY WERE DESIGNED FOR A DOWN-HILL RUN AND THE SPORT AS WE NOW KNOW IT.

ARN IS APPROACHING THE BOULDER-STREWN VALLEY LIKE A HURLED SPEAR. THEN, SUDDENLY, HE IS SAILING THROUGH SPACE!

FOR A BRIEF MOMENT HE IS STARING UP AT THE SKY; THEN HE STRUGGLES TO RISE AND THE SUFFOCATING SNOW CLOSES OVER HIM!

NEXT WEEK :—The Empty Cache.

Prince Valiant

IN THE DAYS OF KING ARTHUR

BY HAROLD R. FOSTER

Our Story: GARM WATCHES IN HORROR AS PRINCE ARN SPEEDS DOWN THE ICY MOUNTAINSIDE AND DISAPPEARS. WITH GREAT SIDELONG LEAPS HE FOLLOWS.

IN SUDDEN PANIC ARN STRUGGLES TO FREE HIMSELF FROM THE SOFT, CLINGING SNOW, BUT IT CLUTCHES HIM LIKE WEAK, SMOTHERING HANDS.

TWO COME TO CLAIM ARN: DEATH AND GARM. BUT GARM WINS AND DRAGS HIS YOUNG MASTER FROM WHAT MIGHT HAVE BEEN HIS CHILLY TOMB.

IN HIS RELIEF FROM TERROR THE BRAVE EXPLORER BECOMES A CHILD AGAIN AND CLINGS TO GARM. IT IS A MUCH WISER AND FAR LESS RECKLESS LAD WHO FOLLOWS GARM TO THE VALLEY BELOW.

HERE, AT THEIR BASE CAMP, GARM HAD PLACED A CACHE OF DRIED MEAT ON A TALL POLE, FOR THEIR RETURN JOURNEY, BUT SIX FEET OF SNOW HAD BROUGHT IT WITHIN REACH OF WOLVES.

THE GREAT STORM SEEMS TO HAVE DRIVEN THE GAME TO SOME DISTANT SHELTER. IN A WORLD OF GLITTERING WHITE, HUNGER BECOMES THEIR CHIEF ENEMY.

LONG AFTER NIGHTFALL THEY COME TO THE RIVER AND THEIR SKIFF. TWO PRECIOUS CROCKS HAVE REMAINED UNTOUCHED, AND THEY FEAST ON HONEY AND BARLEY FLOUR.

IN THE MORNING THE RIVER YIELDS SOME FISH, AND THEY PREPARE FOR THE FINAL LEG OF THEIR JOURNEY HOME IN GOOD CHEER.

NEXT WEEK:—Thin Ice.

HAL FOSTER

1020 8-26-56

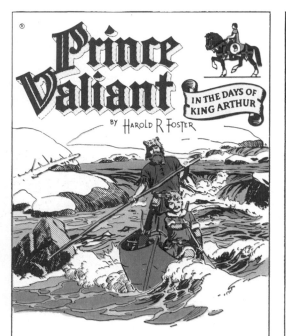

Prince Valiant

IN THE DAYS OF KING ARTHUR

BY HAROLD R FOSTER

Our Story: AND NOW PRINCE ARN'S GREAT ADVENTURE IS NEARING AN END. THE SWIFT RIVER IS CLEAR OF ICE, BUT WHEN THE LAKE IS REACHED, ONLY THE WINDY CENTER IS OPEN.

THEIR SKIS SPREAD THE WEIGHT OVER AS MUCH OF THE SURFACE AS POSSIBLE AND, BY LEANING INWARD, THEY ARE READY TO TUMBLE INTO THE SKIFF WHEN THE SKIM ICE FINALLY GIVES WAY.

THEREAFTER GARM BREAKS A PATH; FOR, THOUGH THIN ICE CRACKS EASILY WHEN HIT FROM ABOVE, IT WILL CUT LIKE A SAW IF ENCOUNTERED EDGEWISE.

THE LONG DAY IS DRAWING TO A CLOSE WHEN THE HUNGRY VOYAGERS AT LAST HEAR THE ROAR OF THE FALLS AND SEE THE WELCOME TURRETS OF VIKINGSHOLM GLOWING IN THE SUNSET RAYS.

SINCE THE PASSING OF THE GREAT STORM, ANXIOUS FEET HAVE TRODDEN A PATH BETWEEN THE CASTLE AND THE LAKE. BUT AT THE CLOSE OF THIS DAY THE VIGIL IS ENDED. BELOW THEM THEIR SON IS BEACHING HIS CRAFT!

IF PRINCE ARN SEEMS TO STRUT A BIT, IF HIS GREETING TO HIS FATHER IS OVERLY NONCHALANT, AS ONE HERO TO ANOTHER, IT MUST BE REMEMBERED THAT HE IS VERY YOUNG!

1021 9-2-56

THEN HE LOOKS INTO HIS MOTHER'S SMILING FACE.....ALL HIS LIFE SHE HAS DOMINATED HIM. IT IS TIME HE SHOWED HER HE HAS GROWN UP! HE WILL....

HAL FOSTER

......BUT WHEN SHE KNEELS IN THE SNOW AND HOLDS OUT HER HANDS TO HIM......?

NEXT WEEK:- The Short Rebellion!

Prince Valiant

IN THE DAYS OF KING ARTHUR

BY Harold R Foster

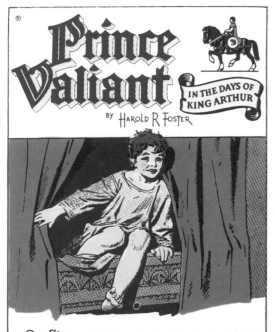

Our Story: AT THE FIRST LIGHT OF DAWN PRINCE ARN LEAPS FROM HIS BED. THIS IS TO BE HIS DAY OF DAYS, THE DAY HE IS TO APPEAR BEFORE THE KING TO TELL OF HIS DISCOVERY OF THE PASS ACROSS THE MOUNTAINS

PROUDLY HE DONS THE CLOTHES HE WORE ON THE GREAT ADVENTURE. THE RAW, UNTANNED HIDES HAD BEEN FINE IN THE SHARP, COLD AIR OF THE MOUNTAINS, BUT IN THE WARMTH OF THE CASTLE THEY SMELL ANYTHING BUT SWEET!

HIS FATHER LOOKS ON PROUDLY AS ARN EXPLAINS HIS MAPS, AND THE KING SMILES INDULGENTLY AS HE TELLS OF HIS TRAVELS. HE WISHES TO PROLONG THIS HOUR OF GLORY, BUT HIS MOTHER BECKONS.

ARN FROWNS AT HIS MOTHER...IS HE TO BE FOREVER TIED TO THIS WOMAN'S APRON STRINGS? WILL SHE NEVER ADMIT THAT HE IS NO LONGER A CHILD? BUT HE FOLLOWS, REMEMBERING HOW SHE PUT DOWN A REBELLION ONCE LONG AGO.

ALETA LAYS OUT CLEAN CLOTHES, TELLS HIM TO TAKE A BATH AND WASH HIS HAIR. "I AM BIG ENOUGH TO TAKE CARE OF MYSELF," HE PROTESTS. "GARM WEARS WHAT HE PLEASES!"

HAL FOSTER

"GARM IS NOT A PRINCE. YOU ARE..... AND CLEANLINESS IS THE MARK OF SELF-RESPECT. WE ARE ALL PROUD OF YOU, BUT IT TAKES MORE THAN ONE SPLENDID DEED TO MAKE A MAN OUT OF A BOY."

1022 9-9-56

"NOW, SON, UNTIL YOUR WISDOM IS GREATER THAN MINE YOU WILL OBEY ME, AND WHEN YOU ARE MORE CAPABLE THAN I, THEN I WILL LOOK TO YOU FOR PROTECTION."

IT IS A MORE HUMBLE PRINCE ARN WHO LEADS GARM BEFORE THE KING. "SIRE, GARM CAN TELL YOU BETTER THAN I THE TRUE VALUE OF OUR DISCOVERY."

NEXT WEEK:— Adventure Calls

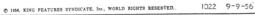

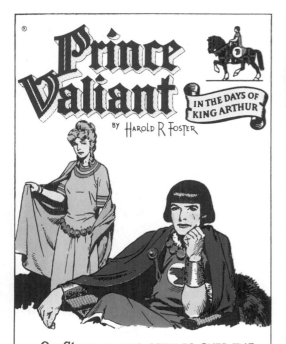

Prince Valiant
IN THE DAYS OF KING ARTHUR
BY HAROLD R FOSTER

Our Story: WINTER SETTLES OVER THE NORTHLAND, AND ALETA WATCHES VAL'S GROWING RESTLESSNESS. THEN SHE REMEMBERS THAT PENTECOST DRAWS NIGH AND AT CAMELOT KING ARTHUR WILL HOLD THE GREAT TOURNAMENT.

ONE DAY A GREAT NOISE IS HEARD, AND BOLTAR ROARS UP, BRINGING TILLICUM AND HER SON FOR A VISIT.

AND FROM ACROSS THE FAR HILLS COMES HAP ATLA, KING OF THE INNER LANDS. WITH HIM ARE HIS WIFE AND SON. IT IS PLANS FOR HIS SON'S FUTURE THAT BRING HIM HERE.

THIS REUNION OF OLD AND TRUE FRIENDS WILL KEEP THE OLD CASTLE OF VIKINGSHOLM GAY FOR MONTHS. BUT THERE IS ALSO A NOTE OF SADNESS.

FOR IT IS THE CUSTOM OF THE NOBLES TO EXCHANGE SONS. THIS IS THE BEGINNING OF THEIR EDUCATION. FAR FROM HOME AND IN A STRANGE COURT THEY ARE TO LEARN COURTESY, SELF-RELIANCE, AND THE WARRIOR'S CRAFT.

WHEN ALETA SEES VAL IN SERIOUS TALK WITH GUNDER HARL, THE ONLY CAPTAIN WHO DARES TAKE HIS SHIP ACROSS THE WINTRY SEAS, SHE KNOWS HE WILL SOON BE GONE.

1023 9-16-56

WHEN THE GREAT HUNGER FOR ACTION IS UPON HIM, SHE KNOWS IT IS USELESS TO TRY TO HOLD HIM. SHE MAKES THE PARTING SWEET, SO HE WILL REMEMBER THE SOONER TO RETURN.

OFF TO CAMELOT AND THE FELLOWSHIP OF THE ROUND TABLE! HARDY FRIENDS, THE ROUGH TOURNEY! AND WHO KNOWS WHAT ADVENTURES MAY TURN UP?

NEXT WEEK :– Camelot !

Prince Valiant

IN THE DAYS OF KING ARTHUR

BY Harold R. Foster

Our Story: LONG BEFORE PENTECOST, THE KNIGHTS OF THE ROUND TABLE BEGIN TO ARRIVE, AND CAMELOT IS A GAY PLACE AS OLD FRIENDS MEET ONCE AGAIN. THESE WARRIORS HAVE WEEKS OF TRAINING AHEAD, FOR THE GREAT TOURNAMENT IS OPEN TO ALL KNIGHTS, AND THEY MUST UPHOLD THE HONOR OF THEIR FELLOWSHIP.

LATE ONE NIGHT A TIRED YOUTH, WHOSE CLOAK SHOWS THE STAINS OF FAR TRAVEL, ENTERS AND HANGS A FAMILIAR SHIELD IN ITS ACCUSTOMED PEG.

KING ARTHUR IS FIRST TO NOTICE IT. "GOOD! THAT LIGHT-HEARTED YOUNG VIKING HAS RETURNED. HE IS THE ONLY ONE WHO CAN HEAL THE GROWING ENMITY BETWEEN SIR GAWAIN AND LAUNCELOT! ALREADY THEIR QUARREL IS DIVIDING THE FELLOWSHIP!"

SIR GAWAIN LEARNS OF PRINCE VALIANT'S PRESENCE THE HARD WAY! WHEN HE GOES TO THE EXERCISE YARD, A YOUNG KNIGHT IN TRAINING PADS COURTEOUSLY ASKS FOR A BOUT.

GAWAIN HAD SPENT THE NIGHT AT THE GAMING TABLE AND DOES NOT FEEL AT ALL WELL, AND HIS NIMBLE OPPONENT GAILY CONTRIBUTES TO HIS UNHAPPINESS WITH MANY A SOLID WHACK.

1024 9-23-56

GAWAIN STEPS BACK. "THERE IS BUT ONE CLOWN WHO KNOWS MY EVERY TRICK, SO TAKE OFF THAT POT, YOU GRINNING FOOL, AND SHOW YOURSELF!"

HAL FOSTER

"OH! WHAT GLORIOUS DAYS AHEAD! DAYS WHEN I PAY YOU BACK TWO BRUISES FOR EACH ONE YOU HAVE GIVEN ME!"

NEXT WEEK:—Tournament Days.

Prince Valiant

IN THE DAYS OF KING ARTHUR

BY Harold R Foster

Our Story: AS THE DAY OF THE GREAT TOURNAMENT DRAWS CLOSE HARDY WARRIORS AND NOBLE KNIGHTS FROM FAR AND NEAR ARRIVE AT CAMELOT AND ARE MADE WELCOME BY KING ARTHUR AND GUINEVERE. SOME GLEAM WITH JEWELS AND ORNAMENTS OF GOLD, OTHERS ARE IN BATTLE-SCARRED ARMOR, AND SOME CLOAKS ARE OF VELVET AND SOME CARRY THE DUST OF FAR-OFF LANDS.

BUT BEHIND THE SCENES....? POLITICS! MANY AN UNKNOWN YOUTH, WHO SHOWS WELL IN TRAINING, SUDDENLY FINDS HIMSELF BEFRIENDED BY A NOBLE CHAMPION!

FOR, IN THE GRAND MELEE UNTRIED KNIGHTS VIE FOR RECOGNITION. SIR LANCELOT CAPTAINS ONE SIDE, DARK MODRED THE OTHER, AND THEIR FRIENDS AND KINSMEN SEEK TO ENLIST THE HARDIEST ON THEIR SIDE.

THE GREAT DAY ARRIVES. WINCHESTER HEATH IS GAY WITH FLUTTERING BANNERS. ALL MORNING LONG THE WRESTLERS, RUNNERS AND ARCHERS HAVE HELD THEIR CONTESTS, AND NOW, TO THE SOUND OF TRUMPETS, THE MOUNTED KNIGHTS PARADE BEFORE THE KING'S PAVILION

TWO LINES OF EAGER YOUNG WARRIORS FACE EACH OTHER. THE KING SIGNALS THE MARSHAL AND HE BRINGS DOWN HIS BATON.

1025 9-30-56

THEN THE AIR IS RENT WITH SHOUTS; THERE IS A THUNDER OF HOOFS AND THE LINES PLUNGE HEADLONG TOGETHER.

NEXT WEEK:— The Challenge.

Prince Valiant

IN THE DAYS OF KING ARTHUR

BY HAROLD R. FOSTER

Our Story: KING ARTHUR GIVES THE SIGNAL FOR THE GREAT TOURNAMENT TO BEGIN, AND A HUNDRED KNIGHTS COUCH THEIR SPEARS AND RIDE HEADLONG INTO THE GRAND MELEE.

EVEN THOUGH BLUNTED WEAPONS ARE USED, IT IS NO SPORT FOR WEAKLINGS, AND THE SQUIRES RISK LIFE AND LIMB AS THEY DRAG THEIR UNHORSED MASTERS FROM BENEATH THE POUNDING HOOFS.

ALL EYES ARE ON A YOUNG WARRIOR IN WHITE, WHOSE STRENGTH OF ARM AND SUPERB HORSEMANSHIP WIN THE PRAISE OF ALL.

FROM THE FAIR HAND OF GUINEVERE HE RECEIVES THE WINNER'S CHAPLET. NOW HE IS DEEMED WORTHY TO CHALLENGE ANY KNIGHT TO A JOUST.

PRINCE VALIANT WATCHES HIM MOUNT AND RIDE SLOWLY TOWARD THE 'COURT OF CHAMPIONS'; AND HE REMEMBERS HOW, LONG AGO, HE HAD WON IN THE MELEE AND THEREAFTER CHALLENGED MIGHTY TRISTRAM.

AND NOW THE WHITE KNIGHT TOUCHES PRINCE VALIANT'S SHIELD WITH HIS LANCE. A CHALLENGE HAS BEEN GIVEN!

NEXT WEEK:—The Shattered Lance.

HAL FOSTER

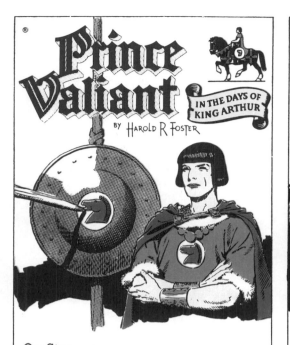

Prince Valiant
IN THE DAYS OF KING ARTHUR
BY HAROLD R. FOSTER

Our Story: THE WHITE KNIGHT IS DECLARED VICTOR IN THE GRAND MELEE AND GIVEN THE RIGHT TO CHALLENGE WHOM HE MAY TO A JOUST. TO THE SURPRISE OF ALL HE RIDES TO THE COURT OF CHAMPIONS AND CHALLENGES PRINCE VALIANT!

ARMED AND MOUNTED THEY MEET IN THE CENTER OF THE LISTS. "UPON WHOM DO I SHATTER THIS LANCE?" ASKS VAL. "WILLIAM VERNON OF LYDNEY," ANSWERS THE YOUTH, "AND MAY THIS SPEAR HOLD FIRM!"

THEN THEY SALUTE THE KING AND TAKE THEIR PLACES, AWAITING THE SIGNAL VAL IS NOT A MIGHTY CHAMPION LIKE LAUNCELOT, GAWAIN OR PELLINORE, BUT HIS HORSEMANSHIP AND DEADLY ACCURACY PLACE HIM AMONG THE CHAMPIONS.

AT THE FIRST CHARGE BOTH LANCES ARE SHATTERED, AND VAL IS AWARE THAT HIS UNTIRED OPPONENT HAS BEEN TRAINED BY A MASTER.

ON THE SECOND COURSE BOTH LANCES ARE AGAIN BROKEN, BUT THIS TIME WILLIAM SUDDENLY SHIFTS HIS AIM FROM THE CENTER OF VAL'S SHIELD TO HIS HELMET. VAL GETS THE SHIELD UP IN TIME, BUT THE POINT CATCHES IN THE SHIELD'S RIM.

WITH HIS SHIELD ARM NEARLY PARALYZED BY THE OFF-CENTER BLOW, VAL CHARGES INTO THE THIRD AND FINAL COURSE. AGAIN BOTH LANCES SPLINTER! A DRAW!

BUT A STRANGE THING HAS HAPPENED... THE WHITE TUNIC IS RED WITH BLOOD, AND WILLIAM, SWAYING IN HIS SADDLE, FALLS TO THE FIELD!

NEXT WEEK:- The Smoldering Feud.

© 1956, KING FEATURES SYNDICATE, Inc. WORLD RIGHTS RESERVED. 1027 10-14-56

1027

Prince Valiant
IN THE DAYS OF KING ARTHUR
BY HAROLD R. FOSTER

Our Story: PRINCE VALIANT AND HIS OPPONENT SHATTER THREE LANCES, AND, BY THE RULES OF TOURNAMENT, HAVE FOUGHT TO A DRAW. BUT THE CROWD IS SHOUTING VAL'S NAME AS VICTOR.

THEN HE WHEELS HIS HORSE AND SEES WILLIAM OF LYDNEY WRITHING ON THE GROUND, A SPLINTER FROM THE BROKEN SPEAR PIERCING HIS NECK.

VAL TURNS TO THE GRAND MARSHAL: "THIS IS NO VICTORY, SIR, BUT AN ACCIDENT. I ACCEPT ONLY A DRAW!"

WITH HIS SHIELD ARM HURT IN THE FIRST JOUST, VAL IS SOON ELIMINATED FROM THE TOURNAMENT. THEREAFTER HE GOES TO THE TENT OF WILLIAM TO SEE HOW SERIOUSLY THAT HARDY YOUNG MAN IS INJURED.

AS HE LEAVES A YOUNG MAID STOPS HIM. "OH, SIR, IS WILLIAM SERIOUSLY HURT? WILL HE RECOVER?" SHE QUAVERS. THEN, MORE MODESTLY, ADDS: "HE IS OUR NEIGHBOR AND MY FAMILY IS ANXIOUS ABOUT HIM!" BUT HER TEAR-WET LASHES BETRAY WHO IS MOST ANXIOUS OF ALL.

WHILE VAL IS ASSURING HER THAT THE WOUND WILL SOON MEND, SIR LANCELOT ENTERS THE TENT TO VISIT THE YOUNG WARRIOR WHO FOUGHT SO GALLANTLY ON HIS SIDE IN THE MELEE.

© 1956, KING FEATURES SYNDICATE, Inc., WORLD RIGHTS RESERVED. 1028 10-21-56

AND ON HIS HEELS COMES GAWAIN, HIS EYES BRIGHT WITH THE ARDOR OF COMBAT. FOR THE VERY AIR IS STILL CHARGED WITH THE EXCITEMENT OF THE TOURNEY.

VAL HEARS THE LAUGHING INSOLENCE OF GAWAIN'S GREETING TO LANCELOT AND SHUDDERS! WILL THE ENMITY BETWEEN THESE TWO BREAK OUT AT LAST AND ENDANGER THE FELLOWSHIP OF THE ROUND TABLE?

HAL FOSTER   NEXT WEEK!—The Gentle Touch.

Prince Valiant

IN THE DAYS OF KING ARTHUR

BY HAROLD R. FOSTER

Our Story: PRINCE VALIANT LISTENS IN HORROR; FROM WITHIN THE TENT COMES THE SNEERING INSOLENCE OF SIR GAWAIN'S GREETING.... COLD FURY IN SIR LANCELOT'S COURTLY ANSWER! UPON THEIR NEXT WORDS HANG THE UNITY OF THE ROUND TABLE AND THE WELFARE OF BRITAIN.

VAL FLINGS ASIDE THE TENT FLAP AND SWINGS THE BLUSHING MAID INSIDE; FOR WELL HE KNOWS THAT LANCELOT'S COURTESY WILL NOT ALLOW HARSH WORDS SPOKEN BEFORE A LADY, AND A PRETTY GIRL WILL OCCUPY GAWAIN'S ATTENTION ABOVE ALL ELSE.

THE LITTLE STEWARD, WHO IS EVER AT WILLIAM'S SIDE, HAS BECOME WELL AWARE OF THE DANGEROUS SITUATION. WITH GOOD-NATURED IMPUDENCE AND SUBTLE WIT HE BRINGS FORTH SMILES AND, FINALLY, LAUGHTER. AND WITH THE LAUGHTER ENMITY FADES.

THEN WILLIAM VERNON FORMALLY INTRODUCES GWENDOLYN BERKELEY. SHE IS SWEET AND SHY, BUT OF READY WIT. SO... VAL SAYS: "IT IS FITTING THAT THE FAIREST MAID AT CAMELOT BE ESCORTED TO HER PARENTS BY THE HANDSOMEST KNIGHT, BUT I WISH TO REMAIN WITH WILLIAM. WILL YOU ACCEPT THE TWO NEXT BEST?"

WITH A PRETTY MAID BETWEEN THEM AND SIR GAWAIN MAKING EVERY EFFORT TO BE FASCINATING, THERE IS NO FEAR OF THEIR QUARREL BEING RENEWED.

© 1956, KING FEATURES SYNDICATE, Inc., WORLD RIGHTS RESERVED. 1029 10-28-56

SO THE GREAT TOURNAMENT COMES TO AN END. THE FEAST OF PENTECOST ROARS TO A FINISH, AND IT IS SAID THERE WERE MORE CASUALTIES AT THE BOARD THAN IN THE LISTS.

HAL FOSTER

AND KING ARTHUR FINDS HE NEEDS A SPECIAL MAN FOR A SPECIAL QUEST, AND PRINCE VALIANT IS SUMMONED.

NEXT WEEK:– *Rumors of Treachery*.

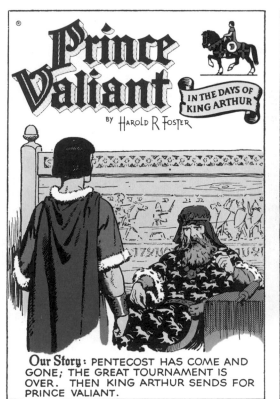

Prince Valiant
IN THE DAYS OF KING ARTHUR
by Harold R Foster

Our Story: PENTECOST HAS COME AND GONE; THE GREAT TOURNAMENT IS OVER. THEN KING ARTHUR SENDS FOR PRINCE VALIANT.

"GO INTO CORNWALL SECRETLY AND FIND OUT IF RUMORS OF TREACHERY THERE ARE TRUE. WE CANNOT SEND AN ARMY UNTIL WE ARE SURE."

VAL QUIETLY JOINS A GREAT COMPANY OF KNIGHTS, THEIR LADIES AND RETAINERS SETTING OUT TO THE WEST TOGETHER.

AND AMONG THIS GAY THRONG VAL FINDS WILLIAM VERNON AND THE FAIR GWENDOLYN. WHEN WILLIAM LEARNS THAT VAL IS BOUND FOR CORNWALL HE INVITES HIM TO RIDE HOME WITH HIM AND TAKE SHIP FOR THE REST OF THE WAY.

AS THE DAYS GO BY VAL FINDS HIMSELF MORE AND MORE IN THE COMPANY OF ALFRED, THE MERRY STEWARD WHO IS SO DEVOTED TO WILLIAM.

ONE STORMY DAY THEY ARE RIDING AHEAD WHEN ALFRED STOPS: "BELOW IS BERKELEY HALL WHERE GWENDOLYN LIVES WITH HER FATHER. ACROSS THE SEVERN RIVER IS VERNON CASTLE WHERE WILLIAM WILL ONE DAY RULE. MAY IT BE SOON!"

1030 11-4-56

HAL FOSTER

ALFRED'S WISH COMES TRUE! HARDLY HAS THE PARTY ENTERED BERKELEY THAN A MESSENGER BRINGS NEWS OF THE DEATH OF THE LORD OF VERNON CASTLE!
NEXT WEEK:— The Proposal.

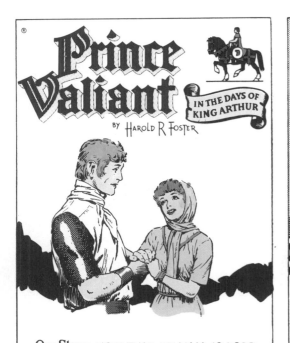

Prince Valiant

IN THE DAYS OF KING ARTHUR

BY Harold R Foster

Our Story: NOW THAT WILLIAM IS LORD OF VERNON CASTLE HE TURNS TO GWENDOLYN, AND FOR A LONG WHILE THEY LOOK INTO EACH OTHERS EYES. THEN, "I GO TO SPEAK TO YOUR FATHER," SAYS WILLIAM.

WILLIAM ASKS SIR BERKELEY FOR HIS DAUGHTER'S HAND IN MARRIAGE, BUT BERKELEY SHAKES HIS HEAD GRIMLY: "YOUR TITLE TO VERNON IS CLOUDED."

"SHOULD YOUR MISSING HALF-BROTHER TURN UP BEFORE YOU ARE TWENTY THE TITLE IS HIS. AND SO, TOO, WILL BE MY DAUGHTER!"

WHILE THE BOAT IS BEING MADE READY TO TAKE THEM ACROSS THE SEVERN THE TWO LOVERS STEAL A MOMENT TOGETHER. TOMORROW THEY WILL MEET WHEN SIR BERKELEY BRINGS HIS FAMILY ACROSS TO THE FUNERAL.

THE NIGHT IS ANGRY WITH WIND AND RAIN AS THE BOAT NEARS THE OPPOSITE SHORE. THEN A BOATMAN SOUNDS A TRUMPET AND, AFTER A LONG WAIT, A FLICKERING LIGHT GLEAMS OVER THE WATER.

"THE OTHER LIGHT!" CRIES THE CAPTAIN, "WHERE IS THE OTHER LIGHT?"

1031 11-11-56

"JAGGED ROCKS GUARD THE HARBOR ENTRANCE," EXPLAINS WILLIAM. "THERE MUST BE A LIGHT ON EITHER SIDE TO GUIDE SHIPS IN AT NIGHT."

HAL FOSTER

FINALLY THE SECOND LIGHT IS LIT AND THE BOAT COMES SAFELY IN BETWEEN THEM. BUT ON THE MORROW THESE SAME LIGHTS WILL DECIDE THE FATE OF VERNON CASTLE!

NEXT WEEK:-The Lost Heir.

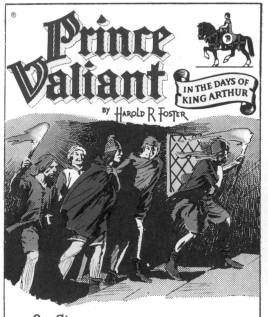

Prince Valiant
IN THE DAYS OF KING ARTHUR
BY HAROLD R FOSTER

Our Story: TORCHBEARERS LIGHT THE WAY AS WILLIAM TAKES PRINCE VALIANT UP TO VERNON HALL. "WE MADE THE CROSSING JUST IN TIME," SAYS WILLIAM, "FOR THE STORM IS INCREASING!"

THE LORD OF VERNON CASTLE LIES DEAD AND ALL IS IN CONFUSION. VAL NOTICES THAT IT IS NOT SOR-ROW BUT A FEELING OF RELIEF, AND HE WONDERS WHAT SORT OF MAN THE MASTER COULD HAVE BEEN. THEN ALFRED, THE STEWARD, QUIETLY TAKES COMMAND AND INSTANTLY BRINGS ORDER OUT OF CHAOS.

WILLIAM PRESENTS VAL TO HIS MOTHER, A PROUD, FRAIL WOMAN WHOSE BEAUTY IS MARRED BY DEEP LINES OF SORROW. "WELCOME TO VERNON, PRINCE VALIANT. MAY YOU BE THE FIRST TO HAIL WILLIAM AS THE NEW LORD OF VERNON."

"OH! MOTHER, I ASKED SIR BERKELEY FOR HIS DAUGHTER'S HAND IN MARRIAGE, BUT HE REFUSED, SAYING MY CLAIM TO THE TITLE IS CLOUDED! IS IT INDEED, MOTHER?"

"YES, WILLIAM, YOUR FATHER'S FIRST WIFE COULD NOT STAND HIS BRUTALITY AND RAN AWAY, TAKING HER BABY SON WITH HER, THE RIGHTFUL HEIR!"

"NOTHING HAS BEEN HEARD OF THEM SINCE BY THE RULES OF SUCCESSION HE MUST LAY CLAIM TO THE TITLE BEFORE YOUR TWENTIETH BIRTHDAY, TEN MONTHS HENCE!'

1032   11-18-56

A SWINEHERD, STUMBLING ACROSS A WINDY BOG, BEARS A MESSAGE THAT MAY SOLVE THE RIDDLE.

NEXT WEEK:— The Hut on the Moor.

Prince Valiant
IN THE DAYS OF KING ARTHUR
BY HAROLD R FOSTER

Our Story: AT THE FIRST FAINT SIGN OF DAWN THE PLODDING SWINEHERD PUTS OUT HIS LANTERN. AHEAD LOOMS THE DARK MASS OF VERNON CASTLE AND HIS JOURNEY'S END.

PRINCE VALIANT FINDS WILLIAM PACING THE PARAPET; "SIR BERKELEY AND GWENDOLYN CROSS THE WATER TODAY TO ATTEND MY FATHER'S FUNERAL. I HOPE THEY START EARLY, FOR THE WIND INCREASES BY THE HOUR!"

A WEARY ALFRED HAS JUST COMPLETED THE FUNERAL ARRANGEMENTS, PROVIDING FOR THE EXPECTED GUESTS AND QUIETING THE EXCITED STAFF, WHEN THE SWINEHERD IS BROUGHT IN.

"I BRING WORD FROM YOUR MOTHER. SHE SAYS: 'BRING ALFRED TO ME. I HAVE NOT LONG TO LIVE AND MY LAST WORDS WILL CHANGE HIS WHOLE LIFE. HASTEN!'"

"MAY I RIDE WITH YOU?", ASKS VAL, WHO HAS GROWN FOND OF THE MERRY LITTLE STEWARD. "THANK YOU, YES," ANSWERS ALFRED, "FOR MY MOTHER IS AN ANGRY, BITTER WOMAN WHOM MANY CALL A WITCH, AND I AM UNEASY, AFRAID."

OVER STONY HILLS THEY RIDE, THROUGH TANGLED THICKET AND QUAKING BOG. A STEADILY RISING WIND MOANS OVER THE WASTELAND.

1033   11-25-56

"MY BOYHOOD HOME!" LAUGHS ALFRED BITTERLY, POINTING TO A DREARY HUT "FIT ONLY FOR PIGS, BUT MY MOTHER WOULD NEVER LEAVE IT."

NEXT WEEK:— The Wasted Life

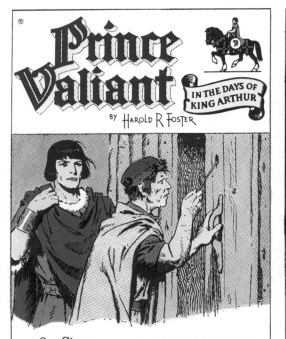

Prince Valiant
IN THE DAYS OF KING ARTHUR
BY Harold R Foster

Our Story: THE LATCHSTRING IS OUT, AND ALFRED TIMIDLY OPENS THE DOOR OF HIS MOTHER'S HOVEL. PRINCE VALIANT FOLLOWS HIM INTO THE DIM INTERIOR, WONDERING.

"COME IN, MY FINE LORDS," CACKLES A THIN, RASPING VOICE. IN A CORNER A BUNDLE OF RAGS MOVES, REVEALING A HAGGARD WITCHWOMAN.

"SIT DOWN, YOU CRINGING SERF!" AND ALFRED OBEYS. "YOU ARE MY MASTERPIECE! YOU, WITH THE SOUL OF A SERVANT, ARE THE RIGHTFUL HEIR TO VERNON HALL! THIS IS THE HOUR OF MY REVENGE!"

IN A VOICE HARSH WITH HATRED SHE GOES ON: "FOR I AM THE FIRST, THE LAWFUL WIFE OF THAT MONSTER, THE LORD OF VERNON HALL, WHOM THE FIENDS HAVE AT LAST TAKEN, AND YOU, LOWLY ALFRED, ARE HIS FIRST-BORN!"

"YES, I WAS ONCE THE BEAUTIFUL LADY VERNON, MARRIED TO A DRUNKEN BRUTE WHO CARESSED ME WITH HIS BOOT AND KISSED ME WITH THE BACK OF HIS HAND. NOW YOU, AN IGNORANT PEASANT, ARE MASTER OF VERNON AND CAN HAVE GWENDOLYN BERKELEY FOR WIFE!"

THEN SHE TELLS THEM WHERE THEY CAN FIND THE YELLOWED PARCHMENT THAT PROVES BEYOND A DOUBT THAT ALFRED IS INDEED MASTER OF VERNON.

"THIS DAY I HAVE DRAGGED THE PROUD NAME OF VERNON DOWN TO THE LEVEL OF A LACKEY!" WITH A WILD BURST OF LAUGHTER SHE FALLS BACK, AND PEACE COMES AT LAST TO A TROUBLED SOUL.

LORD ALFRED OF VERNON HALL AND SIR VALIANT, PRINCE OF THULE, BECOME GRAVEDIGGERS.

NEXT WEEK:— The Parchment

1034   12-2-56

Prince Valiant

IN THE DAYS OF KING ARTHUR

BY Harold R Foster

Our Story: PRINCE VALIANT HELPS ALFRED BURY HIS MOTHER. SHE WHO WAS ONCE THE LOVELY MISTRESS OF VERNON FINDS REST AT LAST, AND THE HOVEL, WHERE FOR THIRTY YEARS SHE HAD PLANNED HER REVENGE, BECOMES HER FUNERAL PYRE.

THEY RIDE THE WINDY MOOR IN SILENCE. THEN ALFRED THROWS BACK HIS HEAD WITH A BITTER LAUGH. "I AM MASTER OF VERNON WHERE ONCE I WAS A LACKEY. WHAT A SWEET REVENGE MY MOTHER PLANNED. THE NOBLE PEOPLE OF THE CASTLE MUST NOW GIVE DEFERENCE TO ONE WHO IS THEIR FORMER SERVANT!"

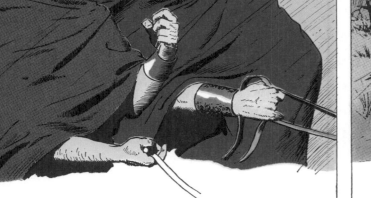

"YES, SERVANT TO MY OWN UNLAMENTED FATHER, TAKING HIS KICKS AND CURSES. WILL I, FROM FORCE OF HABIT, CRINGE BEFORE MY PROUD GUESTS AND SERVE THEM AT THE TABLE?"

THERE IS A SOB IN HIS VOICE AS HE BURIES HIS FACE IN HIS HANDS. "AND GWENDOLYN! I CAN HAVE GWENDOLYN AS MY WIFE, FOR HER FATHER CARES ONLY FOR WEALTH AND TITLE. I HAVE LOVED HER FROM CHILDHOOD, LIKE A DOG, WITHOUT HOPE. BUT NOW.......!" AND HE PATS THE RUSTLING PARCHMENT TO HIS BREAST.

IT IS NEARLY DARK WHEN THEY REACH THE CASTLE AND ALFRED TAKES VAL'S CLOAK. "SEE," HE WHISPERS, "ONCE A LACKEY ALWAYS A LACKEY!"

A SERVANT ENTERS TO LIGHT THE LAMPS. "THE BOAT FROM BERKELEY HAS JUST BEEN SIGHTED," HE ANNOUNCES.

1035   12-9-56

WILLIAM IS PACING THE RAMPARTS ANXIOUSLY. "OH, WHY DID THEY NOT START EARLIER," HE CRIES. "IT WILL BE DARK BEFORE THEY LAND. THE BEACONS! LIGHT THE BEACONS!"

NEXT WEEK:—The Light That Failed

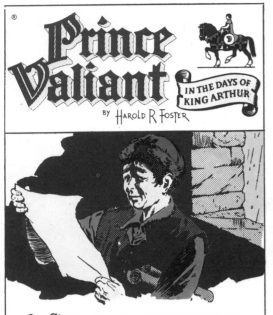

Prince Valiant

IN THE DAYS OF KING ARTHUR
BY HAROLD R FOSTER

Our Story: WILLIAM AND PRINCE VALIANT GO OUT IN THE WINDY DUSK TO LIGHT THE HARBOR BEACONS, FOR GWENDOLYN AND HER FATHER WILL ARRIVE SOON. AND ONCE MORE ALFRED SCANS THE DRY YELLOW PARCHMENT THAT PROVES HIM TO BE THE RIGHTFUL HEIR TO VERNON HALL.

FAR OUT IN THE DARKNESS A DANCING SPECK OF LIGHT IS COMING NEARER... ONLY THE TWO HARBOR BEACONS CAN BRING IT SAFELY BETWEEN THE FANGS OF THE REEF!

ONE BEACON FINALLY YIELDS TO THEIR DESPERATE EFFORTS AND BURSTS INTO SULLEN FLAME. THEN THEY RACE AROUND THE BREAKWATER TO THE OTHER.

THE TINDERBOX GLOWS, BUT ALL EFFORTS TO TRANSFER A FLAME TO THE BEACON ARE DEFEATED BY THE WIND AND SPRAY. "OH, FOR SOMETHING DRY ENOUGH TO CARRY A FLAME," CRIES WILLIAM. "MUST GWENDOLYN PERISH FOR WANT OF THIS GUIDING LIGHT?"

WITHOUT A WORD ALFRED REACHES INSIDE HIS LEATHER JERKIN AND HANDS WILLIAM A DRY, YELLOWED PARCHMENT.

CRUMPLING IT IN HIS HANDS, WILLIAM LIGHTS IT IN THE TINDERBOX AND REACHES THE FLAMING MASS TO THE BEACON. AT ONCE THE OIL-SOAKED FAGGOTS BURST INTO CRIMSON FLAME!

GUIDED BY THE HARBOR LIGHTS, SIR BERKELEY AND HIS DAUGHTER GWENDOLYN FIND SAFETY AT LAST. "BEACON LIGHTS ARE EXPENSIVE THIS YEAR," QUIPS ALFRED WITH A LAUGH THAT CHOKES INTO A SOB.

NEXT WEEK:— The Sacrifice

HAL FOSTER

1036   12-16-56

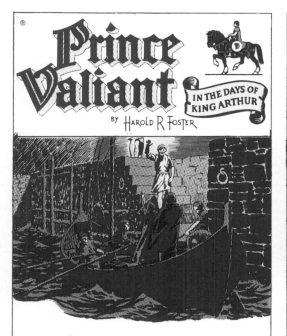

Prince Valiant

IN THE DAYS OF KING ARTHUR

BY HAROLD R FOSTER

Our Story: GUIDED BY THE BEACON LIGHTS, SIR BERKELEY AND HIS DAUGHTER GWENDOLYN COME THROUGH WIND AND WAVE AND CRUEL ROCKS TO A WARM WELCOME AT VERNON CASTLE.

BUT THE PERILS OF THE STORM ARE TOO MUCH FOR GWENDOLYN, AND SHE BETRAYS HER HEART BY FLYING INTO WILLIAM'S ARMS.

ALFRED REMAINS BY THE BEACON HE HAS LIT WITH AN OLD PARCHMENT. HIS TRAGIC EYES FOLLOW THE HAPPY GROUP WENDING ITS WAY TO THE SHELTER OF VERNON HALL.

A NOBLE GESTURE! HE HAS BURNED HIS TITLE TO LIGHT THE BEACON THAT SAVED THE LIFE OF THE GIRL HE LOVES . . . . . SO SHE MAY BECOME THE BRIDE OF SOMEONE ELSE! AND ALFRED, WHO MIGHT HAVE BEEN UNDISPUTED MASTER OF VERNON, IS ONCE MORE NOTHING BUT A LACKEY.

AS WILLIAM AND GWENDOLYN PASS HAPPILY THROUGH THE DOORWAY, VAL LOOKS BACK AT THE LONELY FIGURE ON THE WINDY QUAY. ONLY HE KNOWS THE GALLANT SACRIFICE ALFRED HAS MADE

IN THE CHAPEL THE UNLAMENTED LORD OF VERNON IS LAID TO REST AND WILLIAM IS HAILED AS HIS SUCCESSOR.

ONLY WHEN ALL THE CEREMONIES ARE OVER IS IT KNOWN THAT ALFRED HAS DISAPPEARED, AND A SEARCH OF THE CASTLE GROUNDS IS FRUITLESS.

NEXT WEEK:— The Stowaway

1037   12-23-56

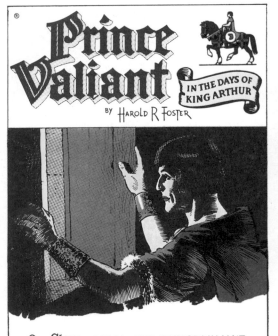

Prince Valiant
IN THE DAYS OF KING ARTHUR
BY HAROLD R FOSTER

Our Story: DAWN, AND PRINCE VALIANT LOOKS OUT TO THE MIST-SHROUDED PIER. WITH A FEELING OF SADNESS HE WONDERS IF GALLANT LITTLE ALFRED HAS ENDED HIS TRAGIC LIFE IN THE COLD WATERS.

TO WILLIAM HE SAYS:- "THERE IS A FAIR WIND, SO IF YOU WILL FURNISH THE SHIP YOU PROMISED I WILL BE ON MY WAY."

A SMALL VESSEL IS MADE READY AND VAL BIDS A SAD FAREWELL TO WILLIAM AND GWENDOLYN, FOR THE LOSS OF ALFRED HAS AFFECTED EVERYONE IN THE CASTLE.

OUT OF THE SEVERN RIVER AND INTO BRISTOL CHANNEL THE WIND HOLDS. THEN THE UNEXPECTED HAPPENS!

THE SAILORS FIND A STOWAWAY! "GREETINGS, SIR VALIANT," LAUGHS ALFRED. "I HOPE DINNER WILL BE SERVED SOON!"

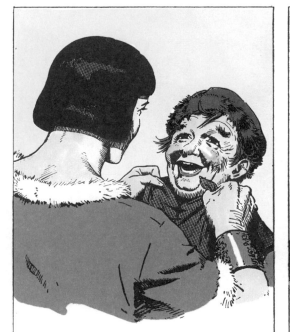

"YOU LITTLE SCOUNDREL!" CRIES VAL HAPPILY, "I SHOULD SHAKE YOUR TEETH OUT FOR THE WORRY YOU HAVE CAUSED!"

"UNHAND ME, FELLOW! YOU HAVE LAID VIOLENT HANDS UPON THE PERSON OF ONE WHO IS OF THE NOBILITY! THIS CALLS FOR BLOOD! HOWEVER, I'LL SETTLE FOR A GOBLET OF WINE!"

BY THE TIME THEY SEE TINTAGEL LOOMING THROUGH THE MIST AND RAIN, IT HAS BEEN AGREED THAT ALFRED WILL BEGIN HIS NEW LIFE AS VAL'S SQUIRE.

NEXT WEEK:- Rumors

1038   12-30-56

Prince Valiant
IN THE DAYS OF KING ARTHUR
BY HAROLD R FOSTER

Our Story: SAILS ARE FURLED AND THE SAILORS MAN THE SWEEPS AS THE SHIP COMES UNDER THE FROWNING CLIFFS WHEREON STANDS TINTAGEL, BIRTHPLACE OF KING ARTHUR. GUARDS APPEAR ON THE WALLS OF 'THE IRON GATE' THAT PROTECTS THE TINY HARBOR.

PRINCE VALIANT STANDS AT THE RAIL, HOLDING UP HIS SHIELD EMBLAZONED WITH THE SIGN OF THE CRIMSON STALLION. AT ONCE HE IS RECOGNIZED AND WELCOMED.

VAL ENTERS THE CASTLE THAT WAS A FORTRESS ERE EVER THE CELT CAME. THE BRITON DEFENDED IT, THE ROMAN STRENGTHENED IT, THE SAXON USED IT AND THE NORMAN REBUILT IT. IT STANDS TODAY, GAUNT AND LONELY, ON THE COAST OF CORNWALL.

VAL HAD HOPED TO GET DEFINITE INFORMATION ABOUT TREACHERY AMONG THE THREE KINGS OF CORNWALL, BUT THE KNIGHTS HE TALKS WITH HAVE ONLY RUMORS.

"ALL WE KNOW IS THAT THE SHIPS OF FIERCE RAIDERS COME TO THEIR SHORES IN GREAT NUMBERS AND ARE WELCOMED. YET THE KINGS WILL NOT LET ARTHUR'S KNIGHTS WITHIN THEIR BORDERS."

VAL TELLS ALFRED OF HIS DIFFICULTIES AND, WITH GRINNING IMPUDENCE, HIS NEW SQUIRE SPEAKS THUS: "FAR BE IT FOR A LOWLY SQUIRE TO ADVISE SO ILLUSTRIOUS A MASTER, BUT OFTTIMES A GREAT WARRIOR TAKES TOO MANY BLOWS ON THE HEAD, AND A CLEVER SQUIRE MAY HAVE TO HELP HIM WITH HIS THINKING. I THINK THAT CASTLES ARE BUILT TO KEEP OUT ARMED MEN, BUT GATES ALWAYS OPEN TO CLOWNS, JONGLEURS, PALMERS, JUGGLERS AND STORY TELLERS!"

NEXT WEEK:- **The Story Tellers**

HAL FOSTER

1039   1-6-57

Prince Valiant
IN THE DAYS OF KING ARTHUR
BY HAROLD FOSTER

Our Story: NOW THE TIME HAS COME FOR PRINCE VALIANT TO ENTER THE FORBIDDEN KINGDOMS OF THE THREE KINGS OF CORNWALL, TO DISCOVER IF TREACHERY IS AFOOT. ONCE BEFORE HE HAD PERFORMED THIS SAME MISSION: —

DISGUISED AS A WANDERING MINSTREL HE HAD ENTERTAINED, LISTENED AND SPREAD RUMORS WITH SUCH SUCCESS.......

.......THAT THE TREACHEROUS KINGS TURNED ON THEIR ALLIES, THE SAXONS, AND THE BATTLES THAT FOLLOWED LEFT BOTH SIDES TOO WEAK TO MENACE KING ARTHUR.

"FETCH ME A TATTERED CLOAK AND MY LUTE!" CRIES VAL. "I WOULD BE A TROUBADOR AGAIN!" "NAY, MASTER," ANSWERS ALFRED, "IT IS NOT ARTISTIC TO REPEAT THE SAME PERFORMANCE, ESPECIALLY WHEN THE THREE KINGS REMEMBER A CERTAIN MINSTREL WHO UPSET THEIR APPLECART!"

"SIT DOWN, LAD," ORDERS HIS HUMBLE SQUIRE. "IT IS MY SUPERIOR JUDGMENT THAT A MIDDLE-AGED PALMER, TELLING TALES OF ADVENTURES IN THE HOLY LAND, WILL NOT BE SUSPECTED OF MEDDLING IN AFFAIRS OF STATE."

WHEN VAL SEES WHAT ALFRED'S SCISSORS HAVE DONE TO HIS MANLY BEAUTY HE MUST BE FORGIVEN FOR A SLIGHT SHOW OF TEMPER!

AS VAL HAS MADE THE PILGRIMAGE TO THE HOLY LAND HE IS A PALMER AND ENTITLED TO WEAR THE CROSS OR CROSSED PALMS. THE PALMER IS ASSURED A WELCOME ANYWHERE AMONG CHRISTIANS.

THEY LEAVE TINTAGEL BOLDLY, EVEN THOUGH THEY KNOW FULL WELL THAT SPIES ARE WATCHING.

NEXT WEEK:— King Durwin.

1040   1-13-57

Prince Valiant

IN THE DAYS OF KING ARTHUR
BY Harold R Foster

Our Story : THREE KINGS OF CORNWALL HAVE CLOSED THEIR BORDERS TO KING ARTHUR'S KNIGHTS. COULD THAT MEAN TREACHERY IS AFOOT? PRINCE VALIANT AND ALFRED BEGIN THEIR PERILOUS JOURNEY INTO THESE FORBIDDEN LANDS TO FIND OUT.

SO THEY ARE NOT SURPRISED WHEN THEY ARE STOPPED BY BORDER GUARDS AND ORDERED TO TURN BACK.

"STOP ME AT YOUR PERIL!" SHOUTS VAL. "I AM A PALMER WHO HAS MADE THE PILGRIMAGE TO THE HOLY LAND AND VISITED THE HOLY SEPULCHER. TAKE ME TO YOUR KING!"

TO THESE SUPERSTITIOUS SOLDIERS A PALMER IS A HOLY MAN. THEY FEAR TO HARM HIM...... LET THEIR KING TAKE THE RESPONSIBILITY!

BY THE TIME LAUNCESTON CASTLE IS REACHED, VAL'S BEARD HAS GROWN, AND NO ONE WOULD RECOGNIZE HIM AS THE YOUNG MINSTREL WHO, TWO YEARS AGO, CAUSED SO MUCH MISCHIEF.

VAL IS EXAMINED BY THE KING'S CHAMBERLAIN, WHO IS EASILY CONVINCED THAT HE IS INDEED A WANDERING PALMER. HIS WORDS HAVE THE RING OF TRUTH BECAUSE THEY ARE TRUE.

104?   1-20-57

BUT KING DURWIN IS NOT SATISFIED: "SEND TO THE CLOISTER AND FETCH THE ABBOT. HE HAS BEEN TO THE HOLY LAND AND CAN TELL WHETHER THE STRANGER IS SPY OR PALMER."

NEXT WEEK: — The Test

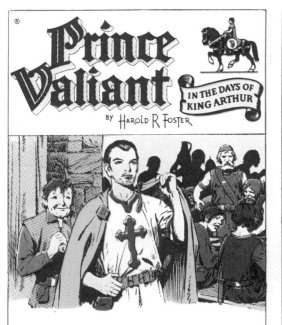

Prince Valiant

IN THE DAYS OF KING ARTHUR
BY HAROLD R FOSTER

Our Story: PRINCE VALIANT AND ALFRED ENTER KING DURWIN'S DINING HALL, ALERT FOR ANY EVIDENCE THAT THE KING IS DEALING WITH THE ENEMY. ALERT TOO THAT THE KING DOES NOT DISCOVER THEIR MISSION.

SEATED NEXT TO VAL IS THE ABBOT WHO, BY HIS PERSISTENT QUESTIONS, CONVINCES VAL THAT HE IS STILL UNDER SUSPICION.

AS THE FEAST NEARS ITS END THE KING REQUESTS VAL TO REGALE THEM WITH TALES OF HIS ADVENTURES IN THE HOLY LAND. HE ARISES CONFIDENTLY AND TELLS THE TRUE STORY OF THE TRIALS AND PERILS OF HIS PILGRIMAGE.

FROM HIS POSITION HE CAN SEE EVERY FACE IN THE HALL. THERE ARE A SUSPICIOUS NUMBER OF WILD DANE, SAXON AND VIKING ADVENTURERS PRESENT, BUT NOT ENOUGH TO PROVE KING DURWIN IS DABBLING IN TREACHERY.

AT THE LOWEST END OF THE BOARD SITS ALFRED, GOSSIPING HAPPILY WITH THE OTHER SERVANTS. A SMALL BRIBE TO A WAITER ASSURES THEM A GENEROUS SERVING OF MEAD. THERE IS VERY LITTLE THE SERVANTS DO NOT KNOW OF WHAT GOES ON AMONG THEIR MASTERS, AND THEY TALK FREELY AMONG THEMSELVES.

"YOUR GUEST IS NO SPY, SIRE. I GAVE HIM EVERY OPPORTUNITY TO TALK POLITICS, BUT HE WOULD SPEAK ONLY OF HIS PILGRIMAGE TO THE HOLY LAND."

ALFRED PRETENDS TO MEND VAL'S TUNIC, THAT HE MAY COME CLOSE ENOUGH TO WHISPER:- "THIS CASTLE IS A PLACE OF FEAR; SPIES ARE EVERYWHERE. KING DURWIN IS A TRAITOR ONLY BECAUSE, TO THE WEST, THERE IS SOMETHING MORE TERRIBLE THAN THE WRATH OF KING ARTHUR!"

NEXT WEEK:- Westward

1042   1-27-57

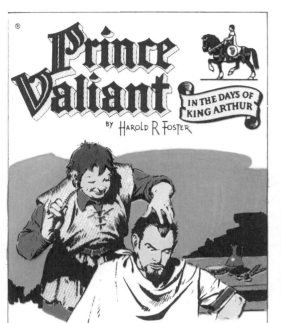

Prince Valiant

IN THE DAYS OF KING ARTHUR

BY HAROLD R FOSTER

Our Story: EACH MORNING ALFRED SHAVES HIS MASTER'S BALD SPOTS AND RUBS CHARCOAL INTO HIS STUBBY CHIN, FOR IT WOULD BE UNHEALTHY FOR PRINCE VALIANT TO BE RECOGNIZED IN THIS DUBIOUS LAND OF CORNWALL.

VAL TELLS KING DURWIN THAT ON THE MORROW HE MUST DEPART, TO TRAVEL WESTWARD TELLING OF HIS ADVENTURES IN THE HOLY LAND, TO ENCOURAGE ALL CHRISTIANS TO MAKE THE PILGRIMAGE.

AND SHORTLY THEREAFTER A MESSENGER RIDES WESTWARD. "NOW, WHY SHOULD ONE HONEST HOST WARN ANOTHER OF OUR COMING," MUSES ALFRED, "UNLESS THEY HAVE SOMETHING TO HIDE?"

FAR OUT ON LONELY BODMIN MOOR ALFRED PULLS UP BESIDE VAL, NO LONGER THE CRINGING SERF BUT SQUIRE AND COMPANION. "SO GREAT IS THE GULF BETWEEN NOBLE AND SERF THAT THE MASTERS TALK FREELY IN THE PRESENCE OF THE LOW-BORN. THERE IS LITTLE THE SERVANTS DO NOT KNOW ABOUT WHAT GOES ON!"

"KING DURWIN WOULD NOT BE A TRAITOR, FOR HIS LANDS LIE NEAREST ARTHUR'S ARMIES, BUT ALL CORNWALL TREMBLES IN FEAR OF THE GROWING POWER OF OCH-SYNWYN, AN EVIL KING FAR TO THE WEST. WITH PROMISES OF PLUNDER HE HAS GATHERED AN ARMY OF FIERCE RAIDERS!"

THE WANDERING PALMER FINDS READY WELCOME. IT IS PILGRIMS SUCH AS VAL, TELLING OF THE WONDERS OF THE HOLY LAND, WHO WILL ONE DAY LAUNCH THE CRUSADES.

IN THE DISTANCE IS RESTORMEL WHERE LIVES THE SECOND OF THE THREE CORNISH KINGS, BUT ON THE ROAD AHEAD STAND ARMED MEN, WAITING!

NEXT WEEK- The Boaster

1043   2-3-57

Prince Valiant
IN THE DAYS OF KING ARTHUR
BY HAROLD R FOSTER

Our Story: AS PRINCE VALIANT RIDES SLOWLY FORWARD, HE MEASURES THE ARMED MEN WHO STAND BARRING THE WAY TO THE DUBIOUS SAFETY OF RESTORMEL CASTLE. IT IS ALL TOO CLEAR THAT THEY HAVE BEEN PLUNDERING IN THE VERY SHADOW OF THE CASTLE.

"I AM A PALMER WHO HAS MADE THE PILGRIMAGE TO THE HOLY LAND," CALLS VAL. "I COME IN PEACE."

"IF YOU GO IN PEACE YOU WILL NOT NEED ARMS OR ARMOR," BELLOWS ONE OF THEIR LEADERS, "AND A CANTING FRIAR SHOULD GO HUMBLY AFOOT!'"

VAL KNOWS HE MUST FIGHT. BETTER TO CHALLENGE ONE OF THE LEADERS THAN RISK BATTLE WITH THE WHOLE BAND..... BUT WHOM? ONE HAS A PROUD FACE; HE WILL FIGHT UNTIL KILLED. THE OTHER IS ILL-BRED AND LOUD; HE WILL BE ARROGANT IN VICTORY, WHINE IN DEFEAT.

"YOU WITH THE VOICE OF THE BULLFROG ...YOU MAY HAVE MY ARMS AND MOUNT," OFFERS VAL POLITELY. "THAT IS, IF YOU ARE MAN ENOUGH TO TAKE THEM!" THEN HE DISMOUNTS STIFFLY AND REMOVES HIS HELMET.

AS HE FUMBLES TO ADJUST THE COIF OVER HIS SHAVEN HEAD, NO ONE WOULD GUESS THAT THIS MIDDLE-AGED MAN IS A HARDY YOUNG KNIGHT OF THE ROUND TABLE.

AS HE WALKS HEAVILY TOWARD HIS CONFIDENT OPPONENT, VAL HAS ONE MOMENT OF MISGIVING.....THE WEAPON HE DRAWS IS NOT THE 'SINGING SWORD'!

NEXT WEEK— *Cat and Mouse*

1044   2-10-57

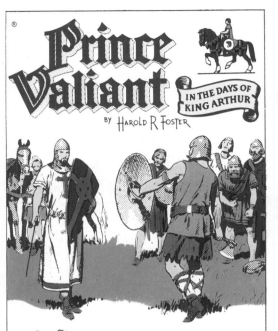

Prince Valiant
IN THE DAYS OF KING ARTHUR
BY HAROLD R FOSTER

Our Story: TO AVOID DOING BATTLE WITH THE WHOLE BAND, PRINCE VALIANT CHALLENGES THEIR LEADER, A MAN WHOSE GREAT STRENGTH WOULD MAKE HIM MIGHTY IN THE PRESS OF BATTLE, BUT THIS IS SINGLE COMBAT.

'THE BULLFROG' AIMS A TERRIBLE BLOW THAT NO SHIELD COULD WITH-STAND..... IF IT LANDED. NOT ONLY IS IT SMOTHERED BEFORE IT BEGINS...

..... BUT THE SAME MOTION OF THE SHIELD BREAKS HIS NOSE. INSTINC-TIVELY HE RAISES HIS OWN SHIELD, ONLY TO FEEL THE SEARING PAIN OF A SLASH ACROSS THE SHINS.

BRUTE STRENGTH IS OF NO AVAIL. CONFUSED BY HIS OWN RAGE, HE FALLS VICTIM TO SIMPLE TRICKS.

THEN HE SEES AN OPENING. STILL DAZED, HE DOES JUST WHAT IS EXPECTED!

THE BULLFROG SEES THE FLASH OF A SWORD, SEES HIS WEAPON FLY INTO THE AIR. BUT DEATH DOES NOT COME TO HIM.

INSTEAD HIS TERRIBLE OPPO-NENT CALMLY ORDERS HIM TO TAKE ANOTHER WEAPON.

REARMED, BUT LESS CONFIDENT, HE RUSHES VAL. ONE TRICK HE HAS LEFT... ...FEIGNING A DOWNWARD STROKE HE CHANGES TO THE UNDERHAND SWING...

....THE STROKE VAL HAS BEEN WAIT-ING FOR. ONCE MORE A SEVERED AXEHEAD SPINS AWAY, AND ONCE MORE VAL STEPS BACK.

COLD FEAR COMES SLOWLY TO THE BULLFROG..... HIS SILENT OPPONENT DOES NOT INTEND TO KILL HIM BUT TO BREAK HIS WILL! IN FRONT OF HIS MEN!

NEXT WEEK:—The Test

1045   2-17-57

Prince Valiant

IN THE DAYS OF KING ARTHUR

BY HAROLD R. FOSTER

Our Story: TWICE PRINCE VALIANT HAS SEVERED THE SHAFT OF THE AXEMAN'S WEAPON, AND TWICE HE HAS REFUSED TO SLAY HIS DISARMED OPPONENT. VAL SEES HIM GRIN AS HE TAKES ANOTHER AXE; THIS ONE HAS AN IRON SHAFT A SWORD CANNOT HARM!

IT IS CLEAR THAT VAL KNOWS EVERY TRICK OF THE AXEMAN'S ART AND CAN END THE CONTEST AT WILL. BUT TO KILL HIM WILL ONLY STIR HIS MEN TO VENGEANCE.

THE BULLFROG BEGINS TO FIGHT WILDLY AS FEAR GROWS IN HIS HEART. NOW HE KNOWS THAT HIS SILENT ADVERSARY MEANS TO KILL NOT HIM BUT HIS WILL!

AT LAST VAL SPEAKS:— "YOU MADE A POOR CHOICE OF WEAPONS.....THIS TIME MY TARGET MUST BE YOUR RIGHT ARM!" THE HARD EYES THAT FOLLOW EVERY MOVE OF HIS HAND FILL THE BULLFROG WITH TERROR. THERE IS NO FUTURE FOR AN ARROGANT BULLY WHO CANNOT HOLD A WEAPON!

FROM A DISTANT HILLTOP THE PANTING BULLFROG LOOKS BACK. NEVER MORE WILL HE BE ACCEPTED AS A LEADER. FILLED WITH SHAME HE RUNS ON.

SWORD IN HAND, VAL WALKS SLOWLY AROUND THE CIRCLE. RIFFRAFF, HARDLY WORTH A SWORD STROKE, BUT HE MUST AVOID A GENERAL FIGHT BECAUSE OF THE DANGER TO UNARMED ALFRED. "CHOOSE A BETTER LEADER," HE ADVISES.

"THAT WILL KEEP THEM OCCUPIED FOR A WHILE!" LAUGHS VAL, AS HE AND ALFRED WEND THEIR WAY UP TO RESTORMEL CASTLE TO PLY THEIR DANGEROUS TRADE OF SPYING.

NEXT WEEK:— **King Ragnor**

1046   2-24-57

Our Story: PRINCE VALIANT RIDES INTO RESTORMEL UNCHALLENGED, A BAD SIGN. THIS MEANS THAT HE IS EXPECTED; THAT A WARNING HAS GONE AHEAD AND HE WILL BE UNDER SUSPICION.

ALFRED IS TREATED WITH CONTEMPT, EVEN GETTING CUFFED FOR HIS CLUMSINESS. FOR HE MUST ACT THE PART OF A DESPISED SERF THAT HE MAY BE ACCEPTED AMONG THE LOWLY SERVANTS.

FOR IT IS ONLY IN THE SCULLERY AND THE STABLES THAT GOSSIP IS UNGUARDED. THE SERF KNOWS NO LOYALTY TO A BRUTAL MASTER, AND ALFRED CAN ASK FOR THE INFORMATION HE WANTS.

VAL SINCERELY BELIEVES THAT ALL CHRISTIAN KNIGHTS SHOULD MAKE THE PILGRIMAGE TO THE HOLY LAND, SO HE SPEAKS WITH CONVICTION. WHO WOULD SUSPECT THIS DEDICATED PALMER OF BEING A SPY?

KING RAGNOR HAS HEARD OF HIS GUEST'S DEXTERITY WITH THE SWORD. HE MAKES AN OFFER: – "WE CAN USE GOOD FIGHTING MEN. STAY WITH US AND WE PROMISE CONQUEST AND RICHES!"

VAL WOULD LIKE TO ASK WHO IS TO BE CONQUERED AND LOOTED, BUT HE MERELY SAYS, "THANK YOU, SIRE, BUT MY SWORD IS DRAWN ONLY IN SELF-DEFENSE OR IN A RIGHTEOUS CAUSE. TOMORROW I LEAVE, GOING WESTWARD IN THE HOPE OF REACHING IRELAND."

"A MESSENGER RODE WESTWARD TONIGHT. AND I HEAR TALES OF TERROR AND OF A MADMAN WHO RULES THERE!"

NEVERTHELESS, AT DAWN THEY RIDE AWAY ON THE LAST AND MOST PERILOUS LEG OF THEIR QUEST.

NEXT WEEK: – The Smiling Monarch.

1047   3-3-57

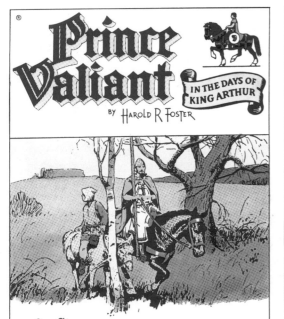

Prince Valiant
IN THE DAYS OF KING ARTHUR
BY HAROLD R FOSTER

Our Story: PRINCE VALIANT AND ALFRED LEAVE RESTORMEL AT DAWN AND RIDE WESTWARD TOWARD THE VERY HEART OF THE VAST TREACHERY AGAINST KING ARTHUR. THEN DOES ALFRED TELL OF WHAT HE HAS LEARNED AMONG THE SERVANTS:—

"THIS KING, OCH SYNWYN, IS A MONSTER WHO WIELDS GREAT POWER. HE HAS GATHERED AN ARMY OF RAIDERS AND ROBBERS, THE VICIOUS SCUM OF THE SEA. THEIR SHIPS PLUNDER THE COASTS AND RETURN WITH THEIR LOOT.!"

"IT IS WHISPERED THAT, WHEN HE HAS RECRUITED SUFFICIENT STRENGTH, HE WILL MOVE TOWARD CAMELOT BY LAND AND SEA. OH, SIR, WE HAVE PROOF ENOUGH! LET US LEAVE THIS PERILOUS LAND OF CORNWALL!"

"WE KNOW TOO MUCH ALREADY. WE ARE WATCHED," ANSWERS VAL. "TO TURN BACK NOW WOULD BRAND US AS SPIES, AND WE WOULD BE HUNTED DOWN. WE MUST SEE IT THROUGH!"

RIDING THROUGH A LAND OF HUNGER AND FEAR, WHERE FARM AND VILLAGE HAVE BEEN STRIPPED AND LAID WASTE BY VIOLENT MEN, THEY COME AT LAST TO OCH SYNWYN'S STRONGHOLD AND SEE A LARGE FLEET AT ANCHOR AND A GREAT ENCAMPMENT.

THEY ENTER UNCHALLENGED AND ARE GIVEN A ROOM.

BEFORE HE CAN BE ADMITTED TO THE KING HE MUST REMOVE ALL ARMS AND ARMOR, EVEN HIS BROOCH, WHICH HAS A LONG PIN!

AND THE KING IS A HANDSOME, SMILING MAN, BUT FOR ONE THING..... HIS EYES ARE THE CRUEL, UNBLINKING EYES OF A SERPENT!

NEXT WEEK:- The Recruit.

1048   3-10-57

Prince Valiant
IN THE DAYS OF KING ARTHUR
BY Harold R Foster

Our Story: PRINCE VALIANT LOOKS LONG AT THE SMILING FACE OF OCH SYNWYN AND SHUDDERS; FOR IN HIS CRUEL EYES THERE IS MADNESS! THE KING SPEAKS: "I AM TOLD YOU WIELD A SWORD AS ONE SKILLED IN BATTLE. I HAVE NEED OF SUCH A MAN."

"FIERCE WARRIORS I HAVE IN PLENTY. I NEED LEADERS WHO CAN PLAN A CAMPAIGN. YOU WILL SHARE IN THE SPOILS OF VICTORY!"

VAL STANDS SILENT. "YOU WILL OBEY MY EVERY WISH," SMILES THE KING, RISING. A SLAVE RUNS AHEAD TO OPEN THE DOORS AND KING OCH CONDUCTS VAL TO A GRIM STONE BUILDING.

RICH TAPESTRIES ADORN THE WALL, A CUSHIONED CHAIR STANDS BESIDE A HEAVY OAKEN TABLE, GLEAMING INSTRUMENTS ARE READY AT HAND. IT IS A ROOM FIT FOR A KING!

VAL IS SICK WITH HORROR AS HE REALIZES THAT THIS IS A TORTURE CHAMBER AND THE KING IS THE TORTURER! A MONSTER!

"I WILL JOIN IN YOUR SERVICE, SIRE," SAYS VAL RUEFULLY. "FOR YOU PRESENT ARGUMENTS NOT EASILY REFUTED. I TRUST MY SHARE OF THE SPOILS WILL BE ENOUGH TO STILL MY CONSCIENCE!"

"SUCH A BEAST MUST BE CRUSHED! MY LIFE, MY VERY HONOR I WILL SACRIFICE TO BRING TO AN END THE AWFUL DEED HE IS PLANNING."

NEXT WEEK –Alias Quintus

1049   3-17-57

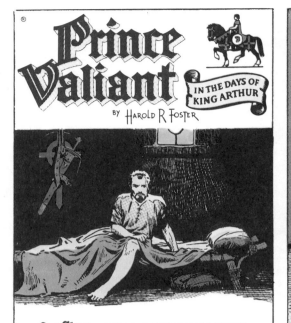

Prince Valiant
IN THE DAYS OF KING ARTHUR
BY Harold R Foster

Our Story: AFTER A SLEEPLESS NIGHT PRINCE VALIANT CLIMBS SLOWLY FROM HIS RUMPLED BED. ALTHOUGH HE IS IN MORTAL DANGER, SOMETHING HE VALUES MORE THAN LIFE ITSELF IS AT STAKE-- HIS HONOR!

AS HE ENTERS THE HALL, A PRISONER, OBVIOUSLY A NOBLEMAN, IS KNEELING, BEGGING HOARSELY FOR MERCY. THE KING SMILES ENDLESSLY, ENJOYING HIS DEGRADATION.

AT A WAVE OF HIS HAND GUARDS SEIZE THE SCREAMING PRISONER AND DRAG HIM TOWARD THE DREAD PRISON WHERE THE KING AMUSES HIMSELF SO CRUELLY.

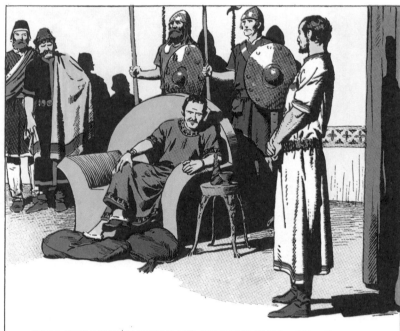

THEN OCH SYNWYN TURNS HIS SERPENT EYES UPON VAL:- "I WOULD KNOW MORE ABOUT YOU. SPEAK!" "I AM A PALMER, I RIDE AT ADVENTURE, A SOLDIER OF FORTUNE," ANSWERS VAL, "MEN CALL ME QUINTUS. NEITHER WEALTH NOR TITLE ENDOWS THAT NAME."

FORTHWITH KING OCH CALLS FOR A SWORD AND KNIGHTS VAL ON THE SPOT: "RISE, SIR QUINTUS, KNIGHT TO KING OCH SYNWYN OF CORNWALL!"

THEN VAL MUST KNEEL AGAIN, PLACE HIS HANDS BETWEEN THOSE OF THE KING AND TAKE THE OATH OF FEALTY. "NOW YOU ARE MY MAN," GRINS THE KING. "TO THE DEATH, SIRE, TO THE DEATH!" ANSWERS VAL.

"TO THE DEATH!" MUTTERS VAL, WHEN AT LAST HE IS ALONE. "BUT YOUR DEATH, KING OCH!"

THEN HE ARMS HIMSELF AND SETS OUT TO DO HIS DUTY TO THE KING.

NEXT WEEK:- A Plan is born.

1050   3-24-57